ARCHITECTURAL GRAPHICS

Third Edition

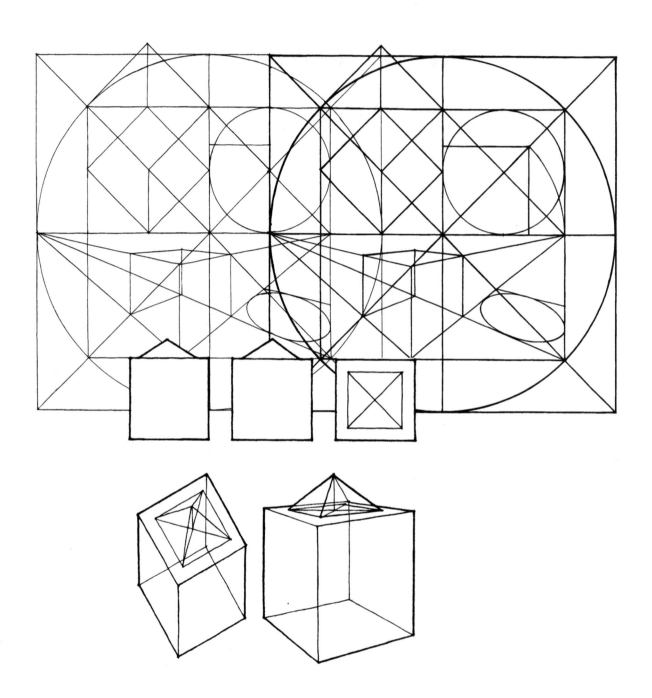

ARCHITECTURAL GRAPHICS

Third Edition

Frank Ching

A VNR Book

JOHN WILEY & SONS, INC.
New York Chichester Weinheim Brisbane Singapore Toronto

Dedicated to my mother and father . . .

Cover illustration courtesy of Frank Ching
Cover design: Stan Hatzakis

Interior Design: Frank Ching
Page Composition: Freeborn Design

This publication is designed to provide accurate and authoritative information in regard to the
subject matter covered. It is sold with the understanding that the publisher is not engaged in
rendering professional services. If professional advice or other expert assistance is required, the
services of a competent professional person should be sought.

Library of Congress Cataloging-in-Publication Data:

Ching, Frank, 1943-
    Architectural graphics / Frank Ching. — 3rd ed.
        p.   cm.
    Includes index.
    ISBN 0-471-28753-9
    1. Architectural drawing.   I. Title.
NA2700.C46   1996
720'.28'4—dc20   95-47551

Printed in the United States of America

10   9   8   7   6   5   4

Preface vii

1 Equipment & Materials 1

2 Architectural Drafting 11

3 Architectural Drawing Conventions 16

4 Rendition of Value & Context 89

5 Graphic Symbols & Lettering 145

6 Freehand Drawing 151

7 Architectural Presentations 164

Index 177

This revision of *Architectural Graphics* consists of a new vertical format and additional drawings that serve to elaborate on and exemplify the principles outlined in earlier editions. It retains the original text, drawings, and spirit of the first two editions and remains an introductory text flexible enough to be adapted to a range of drawing classes and curricula.

The purpose of this primer is to acquaint the beginning student with the range of graphic tools which are available for conveying architectural ideas. The basic premise behind its formation is that graphics is an inseparable part of the design process, an important tool which provides the designer with the means not only of presenting a design but also of communicating with oneself and others in the design studio.

It is important to note here that graphic communication requires mental skills as well as manual dexterity. We must recognize that graphics, the physical end product we are always concerned with, is itself the result of a design process, a careful analysis of why, when, and where a graphic technique is employed, as well as the execution of technique.

Each chapter presents various graphic conventions and techniques and explains the rationale behind their use. The order of the chapters does not imply a specific sequence to the coverage of the material, but rather, it attempts to structure the field of architectural graphics into a comprehensive format.

This text is not intended to be a primer on design or a handbook on sophisticated rendering techniques. No definitive drawing style in emphasized or encouraged. Each of us inevitably develops his or her own style of drawing through practice and experience.

1
Equipment & Materials

Although your own hand and mind control the finished drawing, quality equipment and materials make the act of drawing a more enjoyable experience, and the achievement of quality work becomes much easier in the long run.

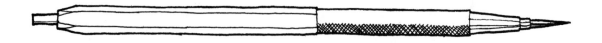

This is the traditional leadholder. Due to its relatively thick lead it is capable of a variety of sharp line weights. The beginner should keep the point well sharpened until the ability to rotate the pencil sufficiently while drawing is developed (see page 14).

This mechanical pencil utilizes a 0.5mm lead, which does not require sharpening. It is capable of consistently sharp, fine lines if you rotate it sufficiently while drawing. For relatively thick, bold lines you have to use a series of lines. Pencils that utilize 0.3mm, 0.7mm, and 0.9mm leads are also available.

The common wood/lead pencil can also be used for drafting. The wood must be shaved back to expose ¾" of the lead shaft so that it can be sharpened like the traditional leadholder.

All three types of pencils are capable of producing quality drawings. Your preference is a matter of choice and your particular skills.

RECOMMENDED LEAD WEIGHTS:

4H · **hard and dense**
- for accurate layouts
- not for finished drawings
- do not use with a heavy hand; grooves drawing paper and may not erase easily
- doesn't print well

2H · **medium-hard**
- hardest grade feasible for finished drawings
- doesn't erase easily if used heavily

F and H · **medium**
- excellent general-purpose lead weight
- for layouts, finished drawings, and lettering

HB · **soft**
- for dense, bold linework and lettering
- requires control for fine linework
- erases easily
- prints well
- tends to smear easily

The degree of hardness of a drawing lead is dependent on:

1. the grade of lead, which ranges from 9H (extremely hard) to 6B (extremely soft);

2. paper type and finish (degree of tooth or roughness): the more tooth a paper has, the harder the lead you should use;

3. the drawing surface: the harder the surface, the softer the lead feels; and

4. humidity: high humidity conditions tend to increase the apparent hardness of the lead.

* Specially formulated polymer leads are available for drawing on drafting film.

The technical pen, capable of precise line widths, can be used for both freehand and drafted ink drawings. As with leadholders, technical pens vary somewhat in form and operation, depending on the manufacturer. Most technical pens, however, utilize an ink-flow-regulating wire within a tubular point, the size of which determines the finished ink-line width. There are a dozen point sizes available, from 5 x 10 (extremely fine) to 6 (2mm).

A starting pen set should include the point sizes indicated below.

───────────────	3 x 10	0.1mm
───────────────	2 x 10	0.2mm
───────────────	1	0.4mm
───────────────	3	0.8mm

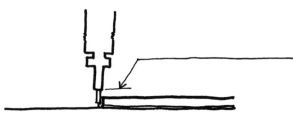

Make sure that the pen you use has a point tube that is long enough to clear the thickness of your triangles and straight edge.

Some points to remember:

1. Keep points screwed in securely to avoid clogging of ink.

2. After use replace cap firmly to avoid drying of ink in pen.

3. When not in use store pens with their points up.

DRAWING INK
BLACK

Use waterproof, black drawing ink. Some brands of good nonclogging ink specially formulated for use in fountain pens are also suitable for technical pens.

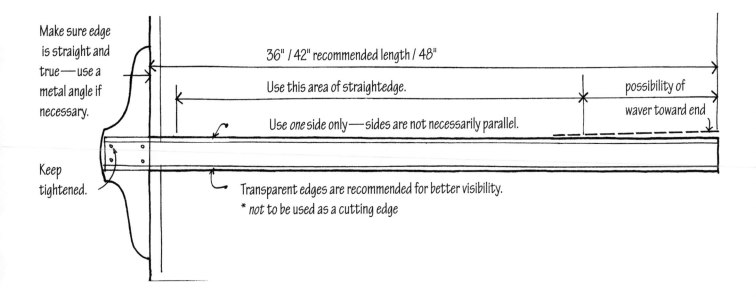

Make sure edge is straight and true—use a metal angle if necessary.

36" / 42" recommended length / 48"

Use this area of straightedge.

possibility of waver toward end

Use *one* side only—sides are not necessarily parallel.

Keep tightened.

Transparent edges are recommended for better visibility.
* *not to be used as a cutting edge*

Although it is relatively expensive, the **parallel rule** is more precise and more convenient to use than the T-square.

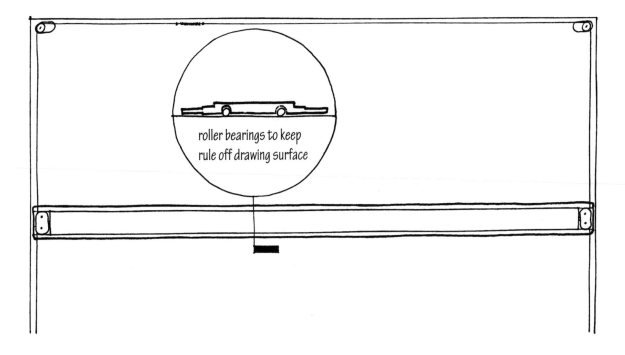

roller bearings to keep rule off drawing surface

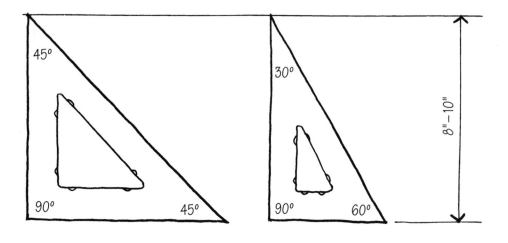

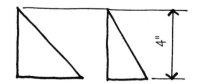

Small triangles are useful for crosshatching of small areas and hand lettering (see page 148).

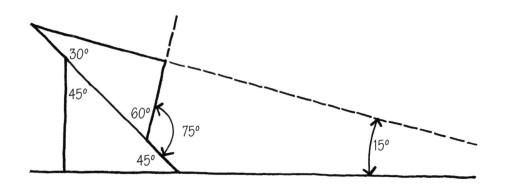

The 45° • 45° and 30° • 60° triangles can be used in combination to produce increments of 15°.

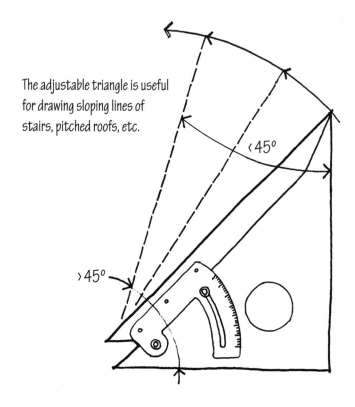

The adjustable triangle is useful for drawing sloping lines of stairs, pitched roofs, etc.

Quality characteristics

- acrylic / nonyellowing
- scratch-resistant
- ease of readability
- good edge retention
- finger lifts

- *Don't use as a cutting edge.*
- *Don't use with color markers.*
- *Do keep clean with a mild soap and water.*

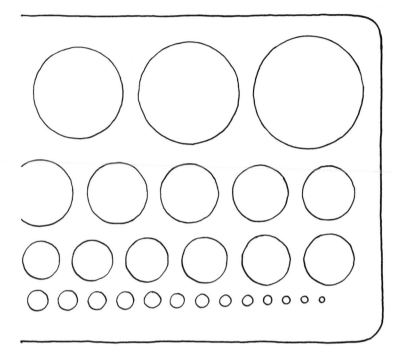

The circle template is a time-saving device useful for small circles of even radii.

Other useful templates include:

Geometric shapes, plumbing fixtures, and furnishings.

For curves of uneven radii use a French curve.

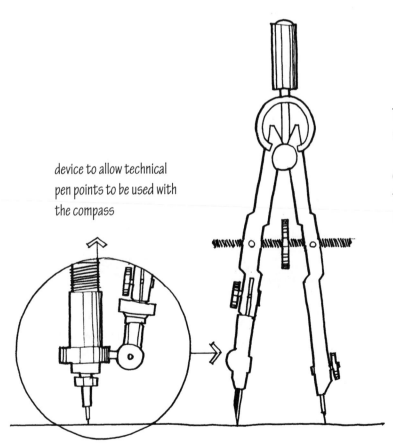

device to allow technical pen points to be used with the compass

The compass is useful for circles of indeterminate radii, large circles, and most ink work.

Care must be taken to match line weights of circles to the rest of the drawing, whether in pencil or in ink (see page 15).

Always use the softest eraser compatible with the job to avoid marring the drawing surface.

Avoid use of ink erasers, which are generally too abrasive for drawing surfaces.

Use pounce powder to prepare drawing surfaces before inking.

Several brands of a soft, granular material are available that provide a temporary protective coating over pencil drawings during drafting. If used too heavily, the powder can cause lines to skip, so use sparingly.

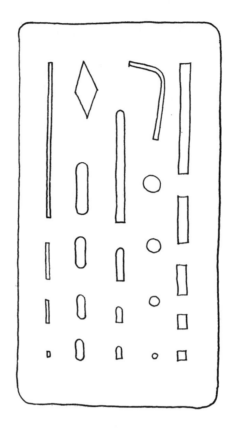

Erasing shield: using one with square holes enables you to erase precise areas of a drawing—also useful to protect drawing surface while using an electric eraser.

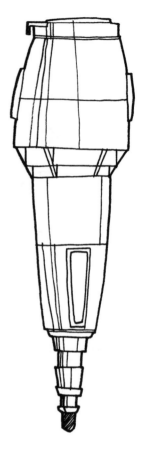

Electric eraser: nice but expensive—useful for erasing large areas and ink.

Drafting brush to keep drawing surface clean.

Desirable characteristics:

- precision calibrated graduations
- engraved markings
- warp-resistant

***not** to be used as a straightedge!*

triangular: 6 sides
11 scales

flat-beveled: 8 scales

flat-beveled: 8 scales

Architect's Scales:

⅛" = 1'0"	½" = 1'0"	¼" = 1'0"	1" = 1'0"
³/₁₆" = 1'0"	1½" = 1'0"	³/₃₂" = 1'0"	3" = 1'0"
³/₈" = 1'0"	¹/₁₆" = 1'0"	¾" = 1'0"	

Engineer's Scales:

10 / 20 / 30 / 40 / 50 / 60 parts to the inch

Metric Scales:

1:100   1:125   1:200   1:250   1:500   1:750   1:1000

Tracing papers are characterized by transparency, whiteness, and tooth. Slick papers are generally better for inking, while some degree of tooth is necessary for pencil work.

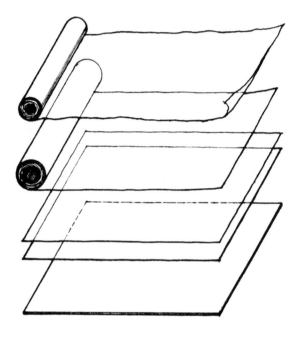

1. **sketch grade**
   - lightweight tissue
   - inexpensive
   - for sketching and quick overlays

2. **medium grade**
   - medium-weight/16-lb.
   - fine or medium tooth
   - for general layouts and preliminary drawings

3. **quality grade**
   - vellum/16- or 20-lb.
   - 100 percent rag
   - for finished drawings

4. **film**
   - 3 to 4 mil clear polyester film for clearest reproductions, permanence, and overlays

Illustration boards are used for finished presentations. 100-percent rag boards, medium-weight or heavyweight, are recommended.

Some brands of illustration boards are more dense than others and white clear through, making them useful for architectural models.

Cold-press illustration boards have more tooth than hot-press boards, which have relatively smooth surfaces.

The following are used to cover drawing boards:

1. Vinyl covers provide a smooth, even drawing surface— Tack holes and cuts heal themselves.

2. Cellulose acetate film laminated to a tough paper base provides a smooth, non-glare surface.

3. A white, *dense* illustration board is an inexpensive drawing surface.

2
Architectural Drafting

The basis for most architectural drawing is the line, and *the essence of a line is its continuity*. In a pure-line drawing, the architectural information conveyed (volumetric space; definition of planar elements, solids, and voids; depth) depends primarily on discernible differences in the visual weight of the line types used.

LINE WEIGHTS:

——————————————— **major/primary**   • cuts/profiles/slices through spaces
HB F/H

——————————————— **secondary**   • elevations/corners/intersections of planes
HB F/H

——————————————— **grid/layout/rendition**   • construction/layout/lines on planes/textures
F/H 2H 4H

LINE TYPES:

——————————————— solid/cut/profile lines

——————————————— solid/elevational lines

– – – – – – – – – – – – dash lines/elements above cut

— — — — — — — dash lines/elements below cut

Note proportion between dashes and spaces between them (⊢⊣ ⊢⊣ ⊢) Keep tight for better line continuity.

———— · ——— · —— centerlines: Longer lines should be approximately equal.

grid lines/grid of centerlines
generally used to indicate a modular or structural system

——— – – ——— · – ——— boundary or property lines

——— – – – ——— · – ——— lines of communication

— G ——— S ——— W — utility lines

LINE QUALITY refers to *cripsness* and *clarity*;
blackness and *density*; and
appropriate weight.

While inked lines vary only in width (unless their value is diluted), pencil lines can vary in both value and width. Thus, a pencil line's weight is controlled by the density of the lead used (affected by grade of lead, drawing surface, humidity) as well as the pressure with which you draw.

It is essential that you understand as you draw what each line represents, whether it is an edge, an intersection of two planes, or simply a change in material or texture.

All lines should start and end definitely, always touching at their ends, always bearing a logical relationship to other lines from beginning to end.

Lines which fade out become arbitrary.

A slight exaggeration at the ends helps to fix a line.

When corners are not met crisply, they appear rounded.

correct

Single-stroke lines are always preferable.

Excessive overlap at corners appears out of proportion to size of drawing.

Corners are critical. All lines should touch one another crisply at all corners.

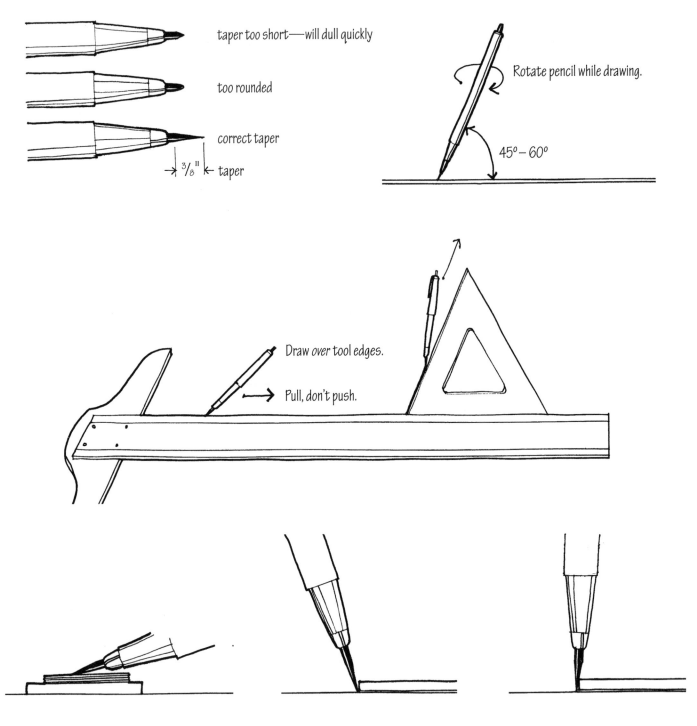

taper too short—will dull quickly

too rounded

correct taper

$3/8"$ ← taper

Rotate pencil while drawing.

$45° – 60°$

Draw *over* tool edges.

Pull, don't push.

If you use sandpaper to sharpen leads, slant the lead at a low angle to achieve the correct taper.

There are some excellent mechanical sharpeners available.

Do not draw into corners—dirties equipment and causes blotting of ink lines.

Draw over straightedge, leaving a very slight gap between the straightedge and lead or pen-point.

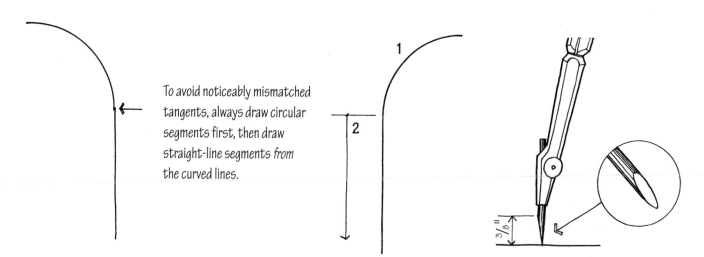

To avoid noticeably mismatched tangents, always draw circular segments first, then draw straight-line segments *from* the curved lines.

A chisel point is recommended for the compass to achieve the sharpest lines without undue pressure—a chisel point dulls easily, however, and must be sharpened often.

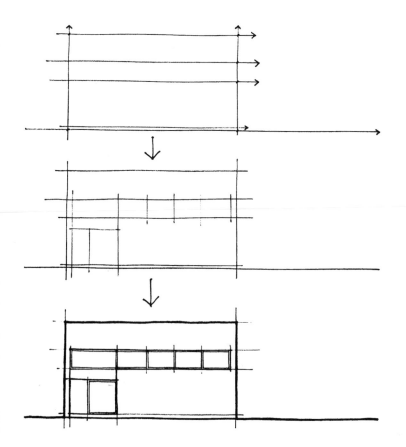

The order in which you should lay out a drawing is:

1. Lightly block out the major horizontal and vertical lines;

2. Fill in the secondary lines; and

3. Heavy up the final lines, keeping in mind the proper line weight of each line (see also pages 20–21).

Do not scrub your lines in; strive for single-stroke lines.

3
Architectural Drawing Conventions

This chapter is concerned with the principal conventions of architectural drawing, their intentions, their capabilities, and their use in architectural graphics. They are considered here in terms of pure-line drawings. The rendition of values and context is discussed in Chapter 4.

Plan / section / elevation views are the primary architectural drawings. They are **orthographic** in nature: The observer's line of sight is perpendicular to both the picture plane and the principal surfaces of the building viewed. Conversely, the drawing surface is parallel to the major surfaces of the building.

roof plan

In orthographic projection, the projectors are parallel to each other and perpendicular to the picture plane.

floor plan

section

elevations

The greatest advantage of using orthographic drawings is that all facets of a form **parallel** to the drawing surface are represented without foreshortening or distortion. **They retain their true size** (to scale), **shape, and proportion.**

In using plan/section/elevation drawings to represent architecture, we
are in fact utilizing an **abstract** method to represent reality.

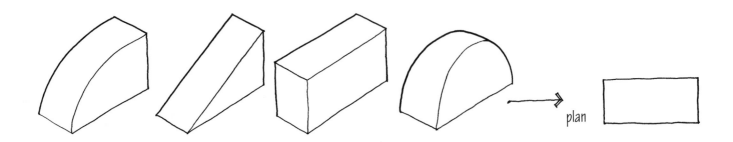

plan

Although the four objects above have different forms, the **plan** views for
all of them (looking straight down) are **identical**. Because of this, the
relationship between plan, section, and elevation views is critical for the
description and comprehension of what we are drawing. When utilizing
plan, section, and elevation drawings to describe architecture, we must
see them as **a series of related views**, all of which contribute to the
understanding of what we are drawing.

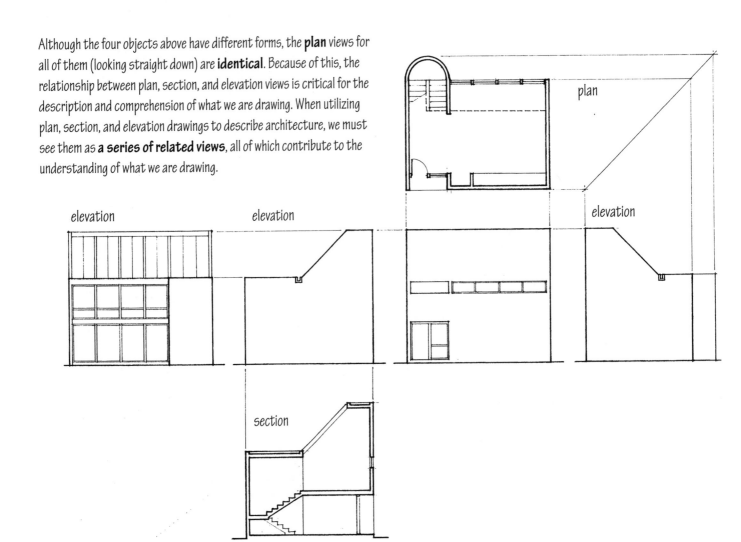

plan

elevation

elevation

elevation

section

The **floor plan** and the **building section** (see pages 34—35) are both sections or cuts: The plan is cut horizontally; the building section, vertically. Whereas in working drawings (for the purpose of construction), plans and sections show the way buildings are put together; in design and presentation drawings the primary purpose of floor plans and building sections is *to illustrate the forms and relationships of positive and negative spaces, and the nature of defining elements and surfaces.*

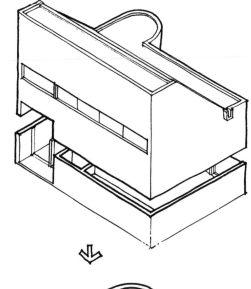

The floor plan is a sectional view looking down after a horizontal plane has been cut through a building and the top section removed.

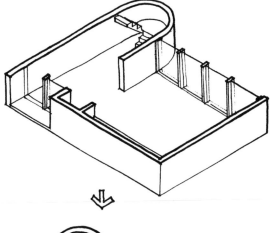

The horizontal section is generally cut through *all major vertical elements* and *all door and window openings.* Usually this cut is about 4' above the floor, but this can vary slightly, depending on what you want to illustrate.

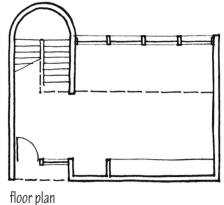

floor plan

Floor plans are normally drawn at a scale of ⅛" = 1'0", or ¼" = 1'0", but for large buildings and complexes the scale can be smaller. The larger the scale of the floor plan, the more detail has to be shown to give the drawing credibility (see pages 24—25).

This series of drawings illustrates the sequence in which a plan drawing is executed. Although this sequence can vary depending on the nature of the building design being drawn, always try to work from the most continuous elements to those which are contained or defined by them.

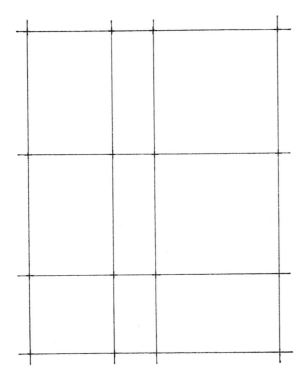

First, the major outline and those lines that regulate the position of structural elements and walls are drawn.

Next, the major walls and structural elements such as posts and columns are given proper thickness.

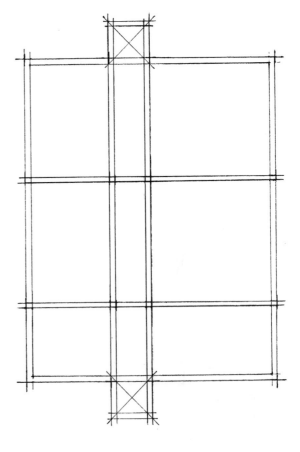

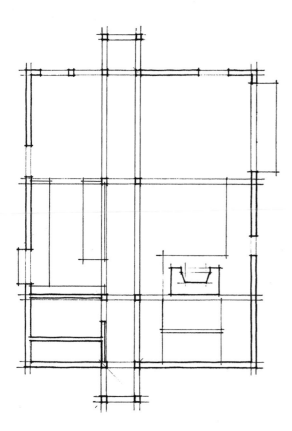

Major built-in elements such as windows, doorways, stairways, and fireplaces are drawn next.

Finally, details such as fixtures, doors and door swings, and stair treads are shown.

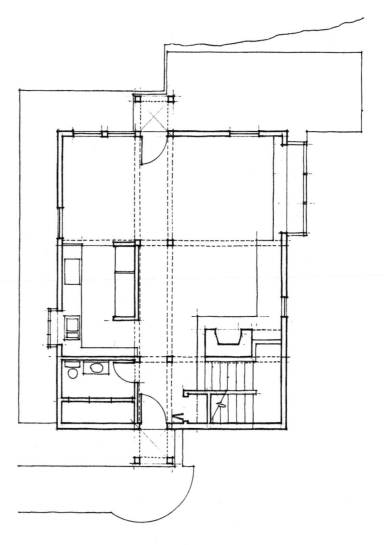

This series of drawings illustrates ways to emphasize graphically the vertical elements that are cut in a plan view of a building. This emphasis is necessary to visually convey the depth of the plan elements and the three-dimensional space being defined by these elements.

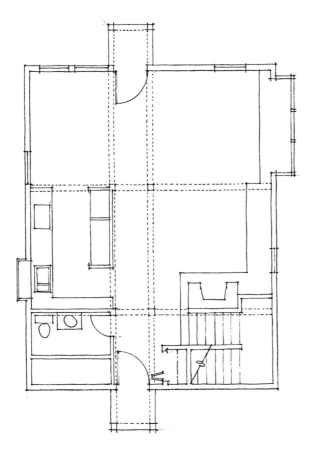

The drawing on the left is a plan view drawn with a single-line weight. The drawing below uses varying line weights to convey depth. The heaviest line weight is used to outline those elements that are cut and therefore closest to the viewer.

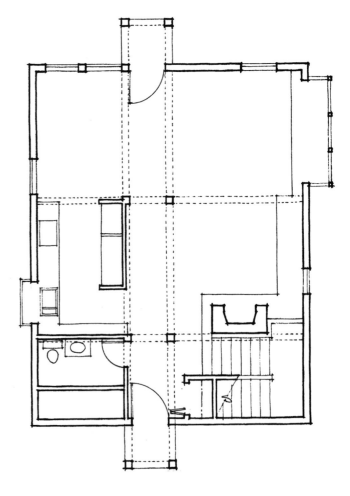

An intermediate line weight is used to outline objects that lie below the plan cut but above the floor, such as a countertop. A fine-line weight is used to indicate surface treatments of the floor and other horizontal planes.

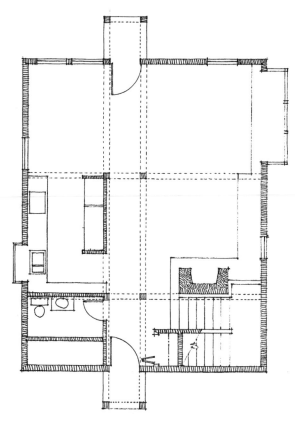

A tonal value or color can also be used to emphasize the elements that are cut in a plan view. If only a moderate degree of contrast with the drawing field is desired, a gray tone can be used to fill in the cut elements.

When other plan elements such as furniture and floor patterns give the field of the plan drawing a tonal value, a greater degree of contrast is required. The cut elements are then rendered in a dark gray or black tone.

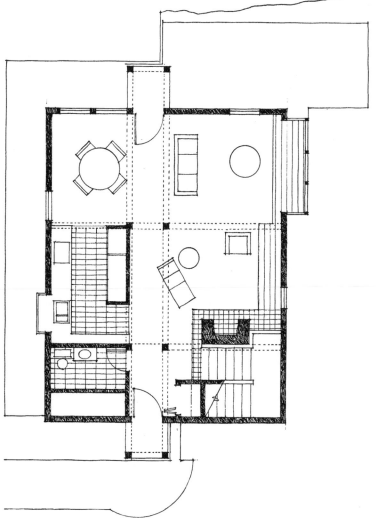

As the scale of a drawing increases, the amount of detail required to give the drawing credibility also becomes greater. This attention to detail is most critical when drawing the thicknesses of those materials that are cut in plan. Careful attention should be paid to wall and door thicknesses, wall terminations, corner conditions, and stair details. A general knowledge of building construction therefore is necessary to execute large-scale plan drawings.

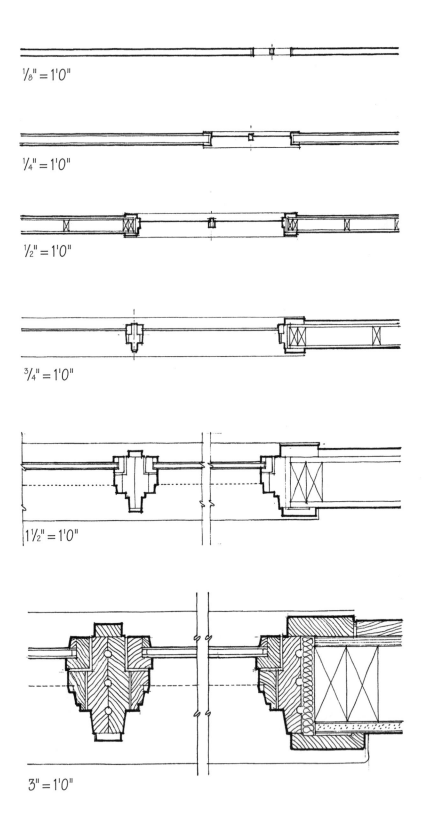

$\frac{1}{8}" = 1'0"$

$\frac{1}{4}" = 1'0"$

$\frac{1}{2}" = 1'0"$

$\frac{3}{4}" = 1'0"$

$1\frac{1}{2}" = 1'0"$

$3" = 1'0"$

Although plan drawings are normally drawn at a scale of ⅛" or ¼" = 1'0", larger-scale plan drawings are useful for the study and presentation of highly detailed spaces such as kitchens, bathrooms, and stairways.

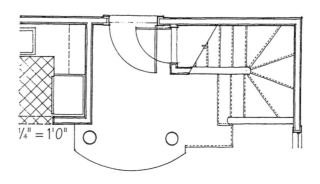

¼" = 1'0"

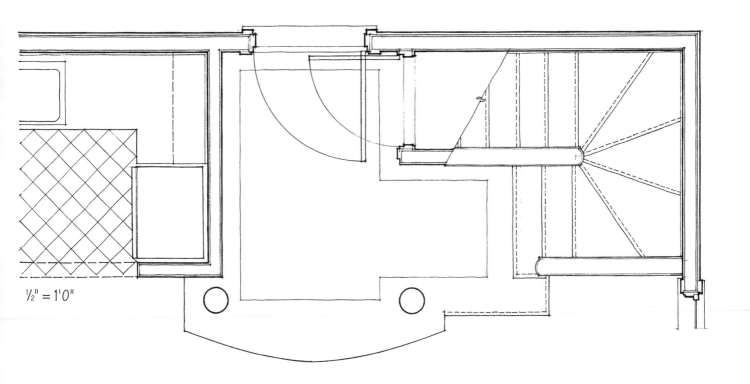

½" = 1'0"

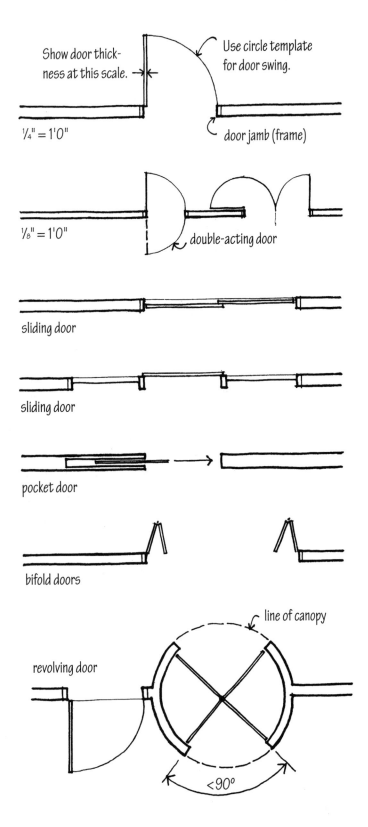

Show door thickness at this scale.

Use circle template for door swing.

door jamb (frame)

¼" = 1'0"

⅛" = 1'0"

double-acting door

sliding door

sliding door

pocket door

bifold doors

revolving door

line of canopy

<90°

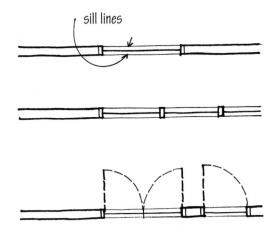

sill lines

- Show normally swinging doors at a 90° opening, as illustrated.
- Note that door swings are shown with light lines and quarter circles.

- Door type (solid wood, wood frame and glass, storefront, etc.) is not illustrated in plan, only in elevational views.

- Window type (double-hung, casement, floor to ceiling, etc.) cannot be explained in plan except for width and location — window type and window height are shown in elevational views.

- Show sill lines with a lighter line weight than walls, jambs, and glass, since sills are not in fact cut through.

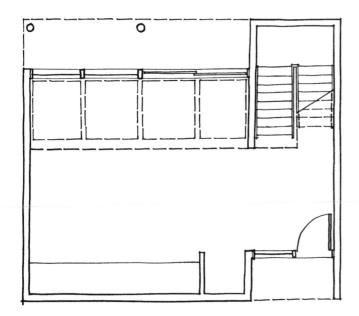

Important elements above the horizontal cut (lofts, sky-lights, roof openings, lowered ceiling areas, roof overhangs, etc.) are indicated by long-dashed lines.

Elements below the floor line are indicated by short-dashed lines,

to contrast with elements above the plan cut, but they are rarely shown.

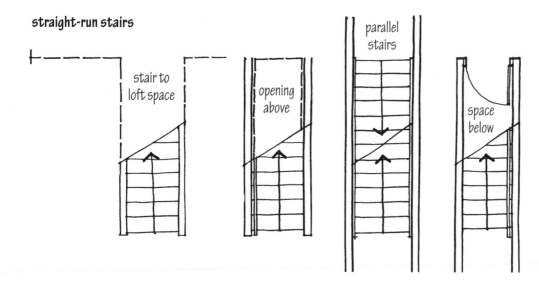

straight-run stairs

stair to loft space

opening above

parallel stairs

space below

U-type (return) stair

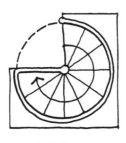

spiral stair

- Show detail such as handrails and toe spaces where scale of drawing permits.

- Convention to indicate direction of stair: Arrow indicates direction (up or down) *from* level of floor plan.

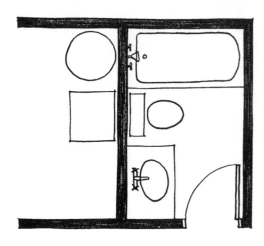

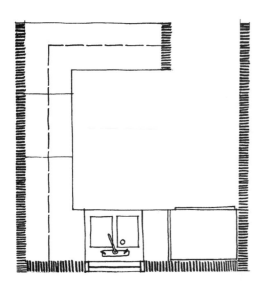

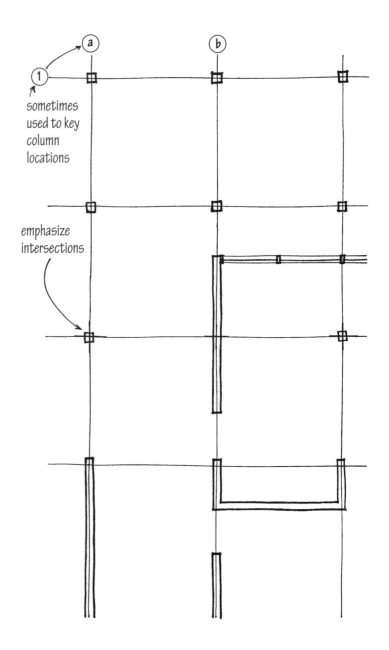

sometimes used to key column locations

emphasize intersections

It should be noted that what is *cut through* in plan (walls, columns, etc.) takes precedence and should be dominant in value; what is seen *within* plan views (flooring, counters, furniture, etc.) should be lighter in value (see Chapter 4 for rendition of values).

A *grid* of centerlines is a convenient and effective means of indicating a structural or modular system.

The grid should be light in value, emphasizing the intersections if necessary.

The **ceiling plan** is conventionally a *reflected* plan of the ceiling so that it has the *same orientation* as the floor plan. It is drawn as if a large mirror were placed on the floor to reflect the image of the ceiling.

Here, as with the floor plan, a horizontal cut is involved, so all major elements that reach the ceiling should be cut and *profiled* with a heavy line.

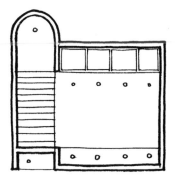

ceiling plan
looking *up* at ceiling

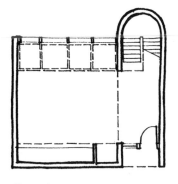

floor plan

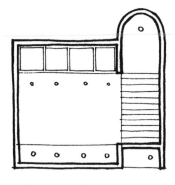

reflected ceiling plan
looking *down* at mirror on floor

The reflected ceiling plan is used to convey such information as ceiling material and layout, light fixtures (type and location), exposed structural members, etc.

The scale of the reflected ceiling plan is usually the same as or smaller than that of the floor plan.

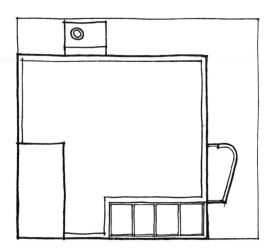

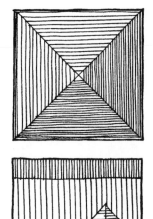

The **roof plan** is simply a view looking straight down at a building, *without any cuts involved*. It is used to convey the overall roof form and massing within the limits of two-dimensional drawing.

When it is part of a site plan and where time permits, it is recommended that you keep the roof plan simple and give tonal value and texture to the site around the building (see Chapter 4).

The roof plan of a building is usually combined with the **site plan**, which is intended to illustrate the location and orientation of a building and the environmental context within which it sits.

The site plan is normally drawn at an engineer's scale of 1" = 20', 1" = 30', etc. but may also be shown at ¹⁄₁₆" = 1'0" or ⅛" = 1'0" if detail requires and space permits.

At larger scales, the floor plan may be combined with the site plan if you wish to illustrate the relationship between indoor and outdoor spaces (see also page 33).

Site Orientation:

assumed north

true north

< 45°

The orientation of a building on a site is indicated by a **north arrow**. Whenever possible, north should be oriented *up* on a sheet. If a building is oriented less than 45° off the compass points, an assumed north may be used to avoid wordy drawing titles (see page 40).

Site Boundaries:

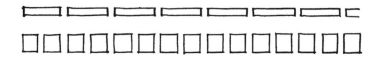

If time permits, a strong contrast in value can be used to indicate site boundaries (see pages 98, 134).

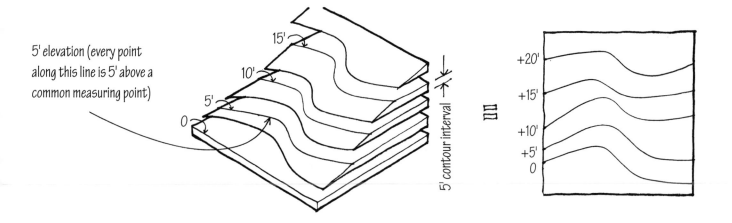

5' elevation (every point along this line is 5' above a common measuring point)

Contours represent changes in topography in orthographic plan drawings by lines of common elevation. With an understanding of contour lines, the viewer can get a relatively accurate idea of the lay of the land from a two-dimensional site plan.

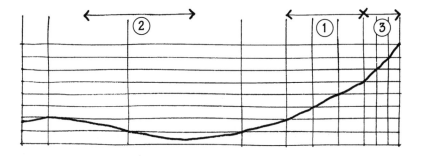

1. Equally spaced contours indicate a constant slope.

2. Widely spaced contours indicate relatively flat or very gently sloped land.

3. Closely spaced contours indicate steeper slopes.

The contour interval is determined by the scale of the drawing, the size of the site, and the nature of the topography. The larger the area and the steeper the slopes, the greater the contour interval must be; conversely, for a small site or one with a relatively flat slope, a 5', 2', or even 1' contour may be used.

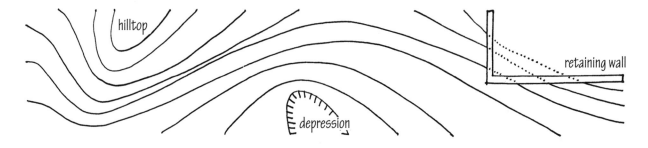

Contour lines are continuous and never cross one another —they coincide only when they indicate a vertical surface.

These drawings illustrate how a building can be related graphically to its site and context. The drawing to the right uses a rendition of the building's roof forms to give it a tonal value that contrasts with the surrounding landscape.

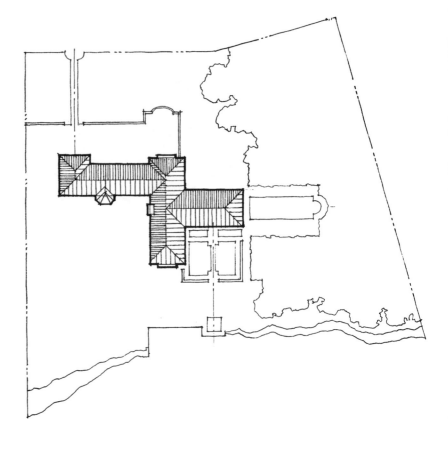

This drawing reverses the value system and uses a darker field to contrast with the building site that is rendered in a lighter value.

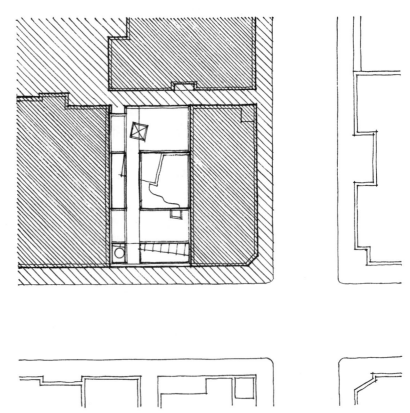

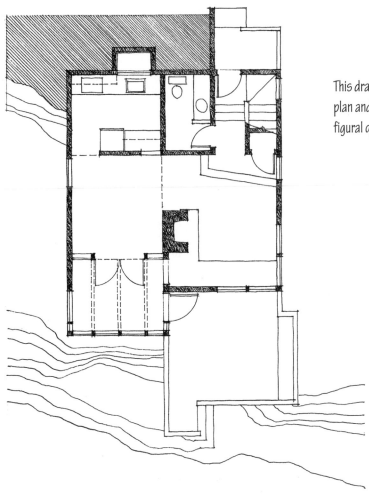

This drawing combines a floor plan with the site plan. The shape of the plan and the dark rendition of the wall elements give the building a figural quality that contrasts sufficiently with its surrounding field.

The drawing on the right illustrates a building whose walls encompass the site; it is therefore a composite floor plan and site drawing.

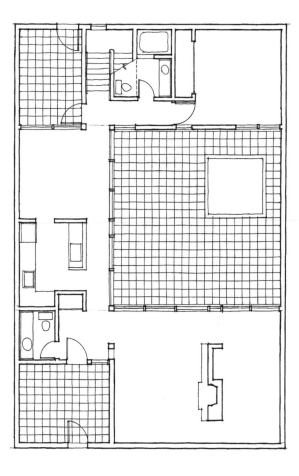

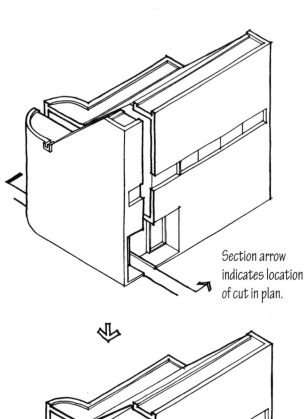

The **building section** is a *horizontal view* of a building after a *vertical plane* has been cut through it and the front section removed.

Design sections, unlike *construction-drawing sections*, should always be continuous, using jogs in the cutting plane only when absolutely necessary. The intent of *building design sections* is to illustrate the greatest number of relationships between significant interior spaces; they look toward the most significant ends of these spaces. One section is usually not sufficient to achieve this unless the building is extremely simple. (Remember that the building section is only part of a series of related views.)

Section arrow indicates location of cut in plan.

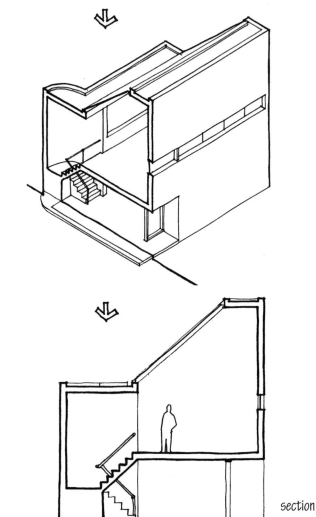

section

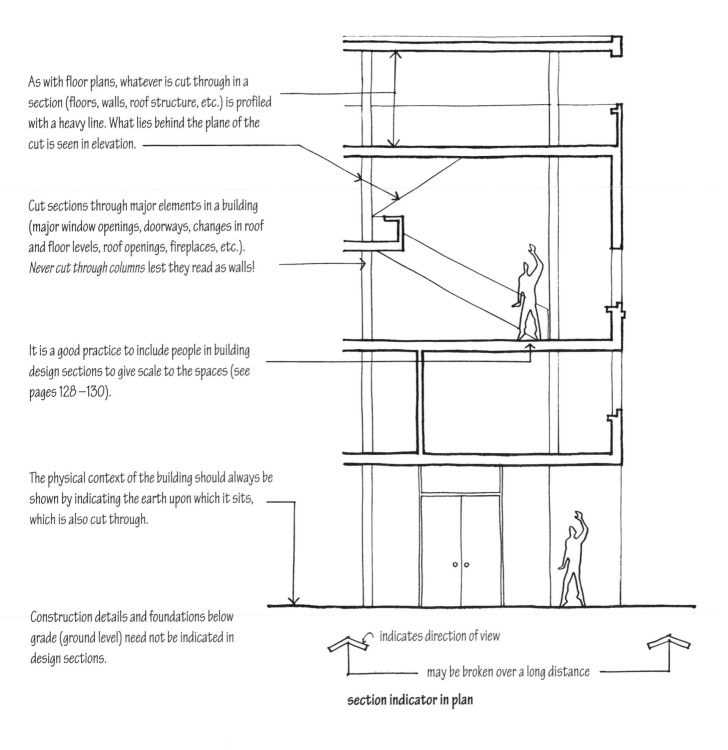

As with floor plans, whatever is cut through in a section (floors, walls, roof structure, etc.) is profiled with a heavy line. What lies behind the plane of the cut is seen in elevation.

Cut sections through major elements in a building (major window openings, doorways, changes in roof and floor levels, roof openings, fireplaces, etc.). *Never cut through columns* lest they read as walls!

It is a good practice to include people in building design sections to give scale to the spaces (see pages 128–130).

The physical context of the building should always be shown by indicating the earth upon which it sits, which is also cut through.

Construction details and foundations below grade (ground level) need not be indicated in design sections.

indicates direction of view

may be broken over a long distance

section indicator in plan

Building sections are normally drawn at $\frac{1}{8}" = 1'0"$ or $\frac{1}{4}" = 1'0"$. For large buildings and complexes, the scale may be reduced to $\frac{1}{16}" = 1'0"$ or smaller. Large scales ($\frac{3}{8}" = 1'0"$) are used only for detail design sections.

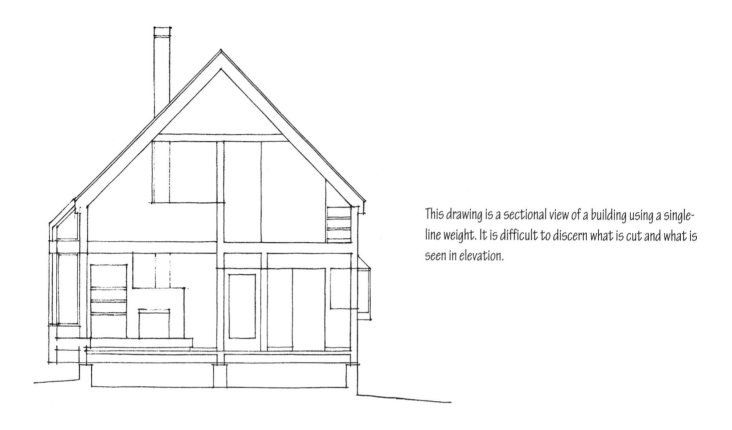

This drawing is a sectional view of a building using a single-line weight. It is difficult to discern what is cut and what is seen in elevation.

This drawing uses a hierarchy of line weights to convey depth in a manner similar to that used for plan drawings (see page 22). Those elements that are cut in section are outlined with a heavy line. Those elements that are seen in elevation beyond the section cut are outlined with intermediate line weights. The further back an element is from the section cut, the finer the line weight should be.

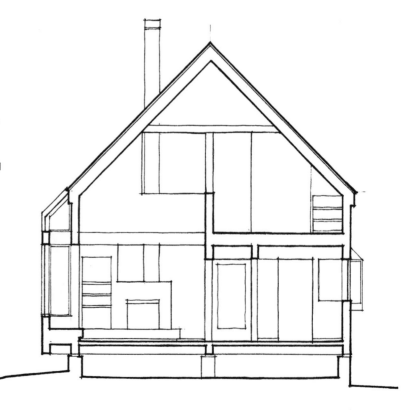

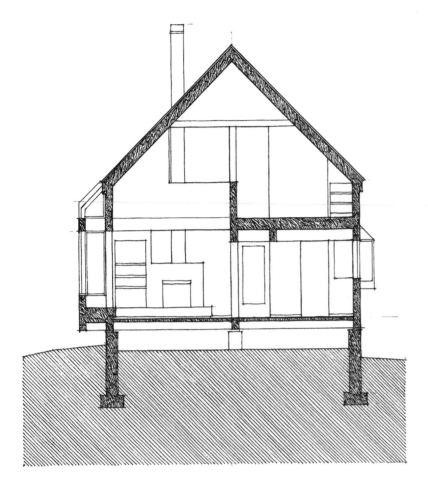

This drawing illustrates how the elements that are cut in section can be given a tonal value to heighten their contrast with elevational elements seen beyond the cut. This is particularly necessary when many elements are shown in elevation.

This last drawing shows how the value system can be reversed when what is seen in elevation is rendered along with the background for the drawing. In this case, the section cut can be left white or given a fairly light value to contrast with the drawing field.

Site sections aid in illustrating the environment and physical context of a building, and the relationship between structures and the exterior spaces they define.

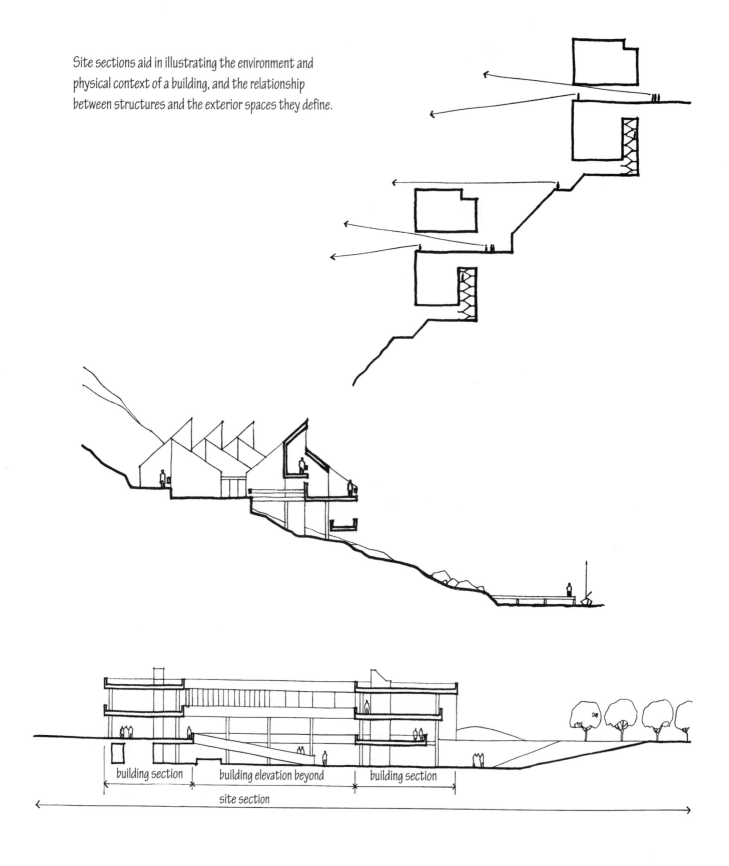

building section | building elevation beyond | building section

site section

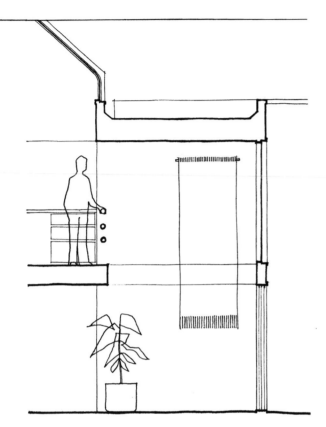

Design section:

emphasis on form and definition of space

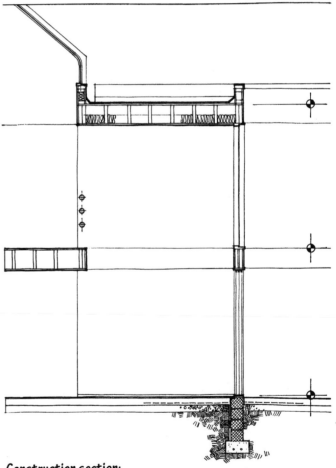

Construction section:

emphasis on building construction details

Architectural elevations of buildings are orthographic drawings of their exteriors from a horizontal point of view. Orthographic projections of a building's interior vertical surfaces, as seen in building sections, are interior elevations.

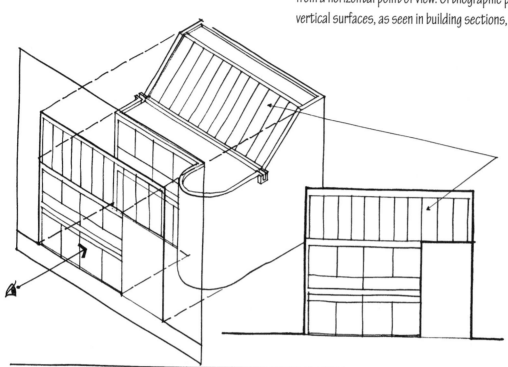

All planar surfaces not parallel to the drawing surface (not perpendicular to the observer's line of sight) appear foreshortened.

All planar surfaces parallel to the drawing surface, and perpendicular to the observer's line of sight retain their true size (to scale), shape, and proportion.

Architectural elevations are labeled in relation to the compass points (see page 30). It is important to note that the face of a building is named for the direction it *faces* or the direction *from which you see it*; e.g., the north elevation of a building faces north or is the elevation you see from the north. In some instances you may label an elevation with respect to a unique site feature; e.g., Main Street elevation (elevation facing Main Street) or lake elevation (elevation seen from the lake).

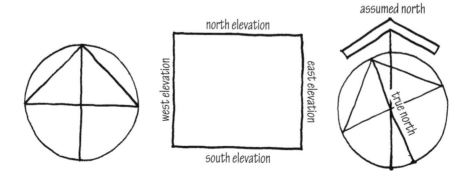

As the scale of a drawing increases, more detail must be shown. Normally, building elevations are drawn at a scale of $\frac{1}{8}$" = 1'0" or $\frac{1}{4}$" = 1'0". Large buildings may be shown at $\frac{1}{16}$" = 1'0" or smaller. For large-scale studies, detail elevations may be shown at $\frac{3}{8}$" = 1'0" or $\frac{3}{4}$" = 1'0".

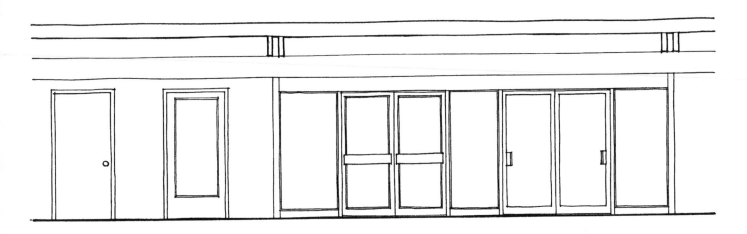

The types of doors and windows illustrated here are not meant to be copied; you must understand the construction of the doors and windows you are drawing and realize that every line you draw represents something in that construction.

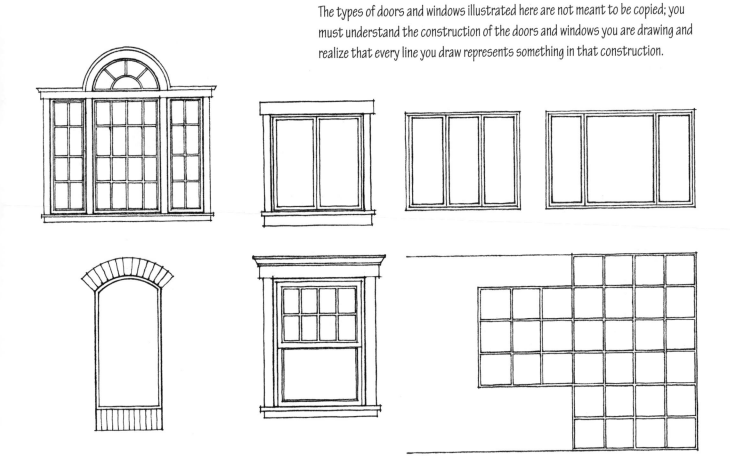

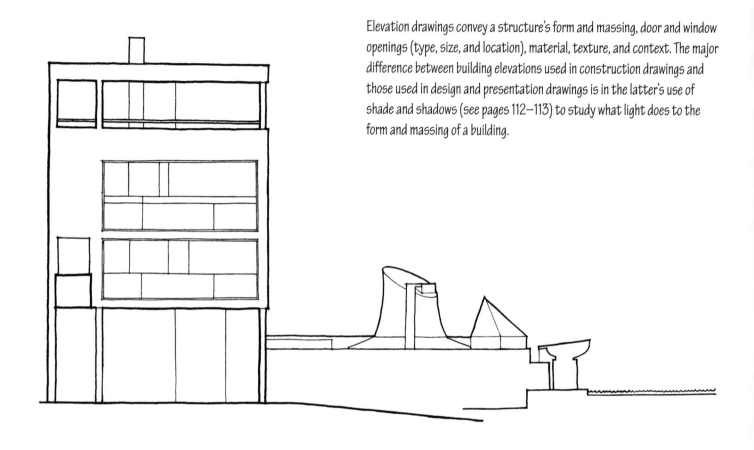

Elevation drawings convey a structure's form and massing, door and window openings (type, size, and location), material, texture, and context. The major difference between building elevations used in construction drawings and those used in design and presentation drawings is in the latter's use of shade and shadows (see pages 112–113) to study what light does to the form and massing of a building.

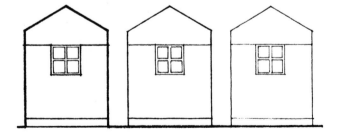

In a pure-line drawing without shade and shadows discernible differences in line weight can aid in suggesting depth of planes. The heavier the delineation of an element, the farther forward it appears; the lighter the delineation, the further it appears to recede. A strong profile line helps to silhouette the building's overall form.

Profile lines should always continue along the ground plane for a distance sufficient to indicate the environment within which the building sits.

Tonal values created by the rendition of materials, textures, and shadows can be used to enhance the depth of an elevation drawing. In this example, the tonal values and the greater amount of detail shown make the right-hand building appear to be forward of the other structures. Additional visual clues that are used to convey depth are the overlapping of the building forms, a slight reduction in scale of the buildings as they recede, and a slight reduction in the line weight and values used to define the background forms.

Reducing the scale of elements in an elevation drawing does not strictly follow the rules of orthographic projection. This technique requires judgement and should not be used if it causes confusion.

Emphasis can be given to a building that is shown in its context by using sharply defined tonal values.

An elevation drawing of a building can be considered a section cut through the ground some distance in front of the building form. This distance will vary according to what one wishes to show in front of the building and to what degree these elements will obscure the building form.

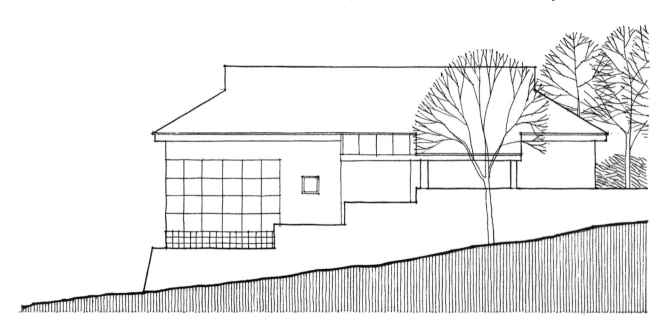

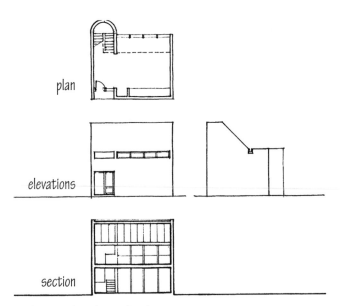

plan

elevations

section

Multiview / orthographic drawings

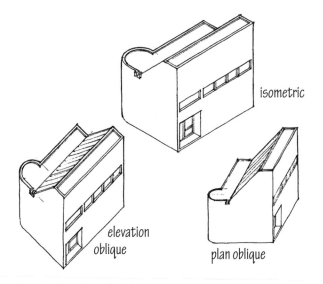

isometric

elevation
oblique

plan oblique

Single-view / paraline drawings

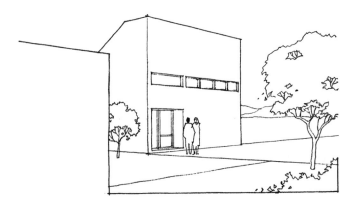

Single-view / perspective drawing

While the orthographic drawing conventions—plan/section/elevation—depict reality through a fragmented series of distinct but related views, single-view drawings illustrate the three dimensions of form simultaneously and thus show form relationships in a more realistic manner. For this reason, the two major types of single-view drawings, paraline drawings and perspectives, are called pictorial drawing.

Paraline drawings differ from perspectives in one major way: Parallel lines remain parallel in paraline drawings, while they converge to vanishing points in perspectives.

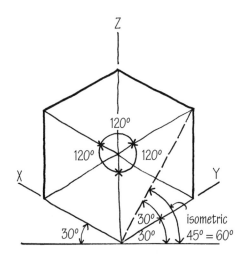

There are a number of paraline drawings, which are named after the method of projection that is used to develop them. Two of the most common in architectural drawing are discussed in this section: isometric and oblique (both plan and elevation).

ISOMETRIC

- All three visible surfaces have equal emphasis.
- Isometric projection is relatively inflexible.
- Orthographic plans and elevations can never be used in an isometric drawing.

PLAN OBLIQUES

- A 45° • 45° oblique has a higher angle of view than an isometric, and horizontal planes receive more emphasis.
- A 30° • 60° oblique also has a high angle of view with one vertical plane receiving more emphasis than the other.

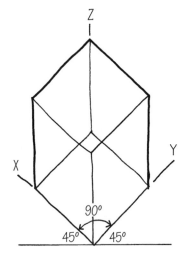

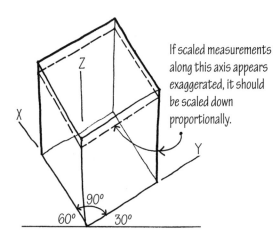

If scaled measurements along this axis appears exaggerated, it should be scaled down proportionally.

- In plan obliques, orthographic plan views can be utilized—this is advantageous in showing the true from of horizontal planes and in depicting horizontal circular planes.

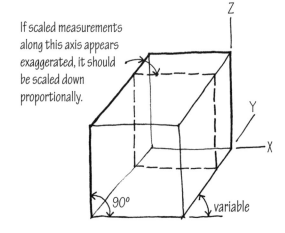

If scaled measurements along this axis appears exaggerated, it should be scaled down proportionally.

ELEVATION OBLIQUE

- A vertical plane remains parallel to the drawing surface, showing itself in true size (to scale), shape, and proportion—this face of the building should be the length of the building, the most significant face, or the most complex.

In each of these drawings:

1. All vertical lines remain vertical.
2. All parallel lines remain parallel.
3. All lines parallel to X • Y • Z axes can be drawn to scale.

Circles in nonfrontal planes in paraline drawings appear as ellipses. With the four-center method (using two sets of radii and a compass or circle template) you can approximate an ellipse that is usually close enough to a true ellipse to suit most purposes.

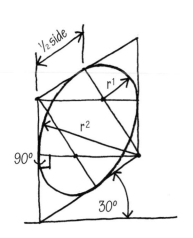

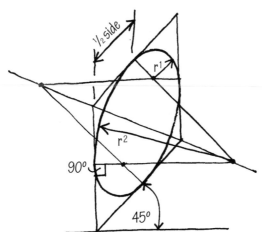

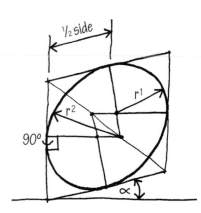

CONSTRUCTION:

1. Draw circumscribing square axonometrically.

2. At the midpoints of the sides of the axonometric square draw perpendiculars and extend them until they intersect.

3. With these points of intersection as centers and with radii r^1 and r^2 equal to the respective lengths of the perpendiculars, describe two sets of arcs in equal pairs between the points where the perpendiculars originate.

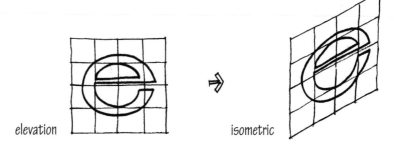

elevation   isometric

For freeform curvilinear lines you can use a grid along the appropriate pair of axes to plot the points of intersection in the paraline drawing.

For most rectilinear forms the construction of a paraline drawing is relatively simple, since all lines parallel to the X • Y • Z axes (axonometric lines) are to scale and all parallel lines remain parallel. Standard 30° • 30°, 45° • 45°, and 30° • 60° orientations for the X • Y base axes also aid in the construction of a paraline drawing.

Nonaxonometric lines (lines not parallel to the X • Y • Z axes) are *not* drawn to scale; the axonometric ends of nonaxonometric lines must first be located, and then the nonaxonometric lines are drawn between these points:

1. Enclose the irregular form in a rectilinear box.

2. Using the edges of this box as measuring lines, locate the ends of the nonaxonometric lines through the use of offset measurements.

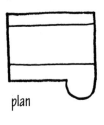

plan

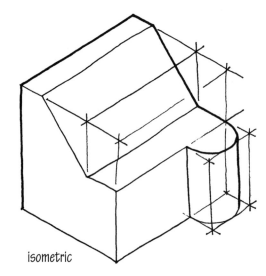

isometric

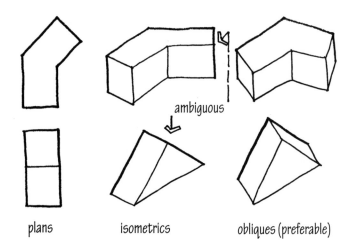

plans   isometrics   obliques (preferable)

ambiguous

The major pictorial defect of an axonometric drawing is that parallel lines appear to diverge as they recede in apparent contradiction to what we normally see in perspective. For this reason excessive lengths in the X- or Y-dimensions should be avoided.

Cubic forms and 45° lines sometimes appear flat in isometric drawings (an optical illusion). In such cases a plan oblique may be preferable.

Paraline drawings are particularly useful in architectural graphics because of their ease of construction (both drafted and freehand) and their effectiveness as a pictorial view. Most people find paraline drawings easy to understand, since they resemble natural perception more closely than orthographic drawings.

The following are examples of some of the ways paraline drawings are used:

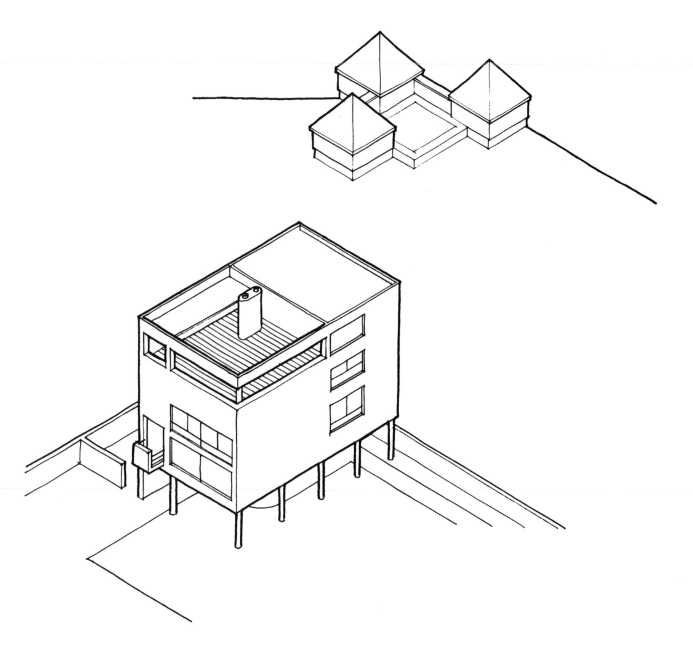

1. **Overall building form, configuration, and disposition.**
    Paraline drawings are always aerial views and thus lack the natural perceptual point of view of which perspectives are capable.

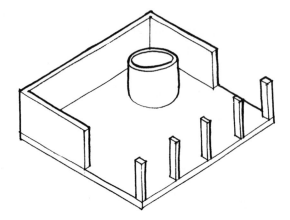

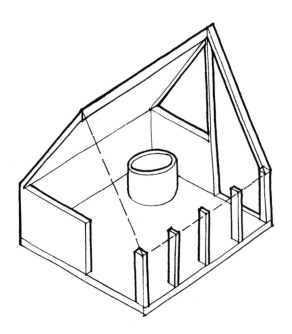

- An isometric such as this can be deceptive, since the walls tend to be read at full height—always draw wall at full height.

- Always indicate the overall form of the building and space within—the less you cut away from the total form, the more comprehensible the true nature of the form is.

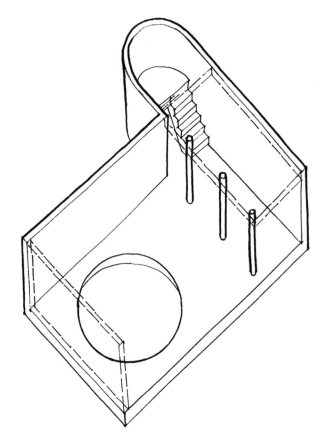

- For circles in plan, it is easier to use a plan oblique than an isometric, since the orthographic plan is used as the base drawing and horizontal circles remain true circles.

2. Building cutaways

These are used to illustrate interiors.

3. Illustrating building details

As with other scale drawings, the larger the scale, the more detail you have to show.

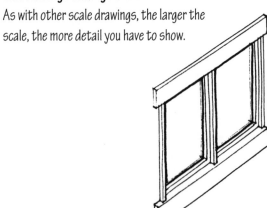

HIERARCHY OF LINES:

1. profile of total field of each floor level—do not profile ground line

2. horizontal-cut lines

3. profile lines of individual elements—edges against space (see page 93)

4. transitions in form (corners)

5. material texture

6. vertical (light or dashed) lines to reinforce vertical relationships of structure/circulation/form

Giving the horizontal floor planes a tonal value or texture aids in the definition of vertical elements.

Any overlap between floor levels should not cover significant information.

4. **Expanded views** are especially useful in illustrating vertical relationships in multistory buildings.

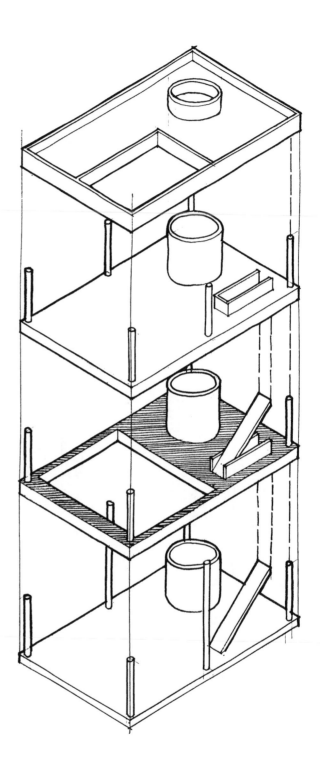

A building form can also be expanded along the X• Y • Z axes of a paraline drawing to illustrate how its construction components relate to one another and/or to selectively reveal the interior spaces within. Another method for revealing an interior space without removing any building elements is to draw the defining elements so that they appear transparent.

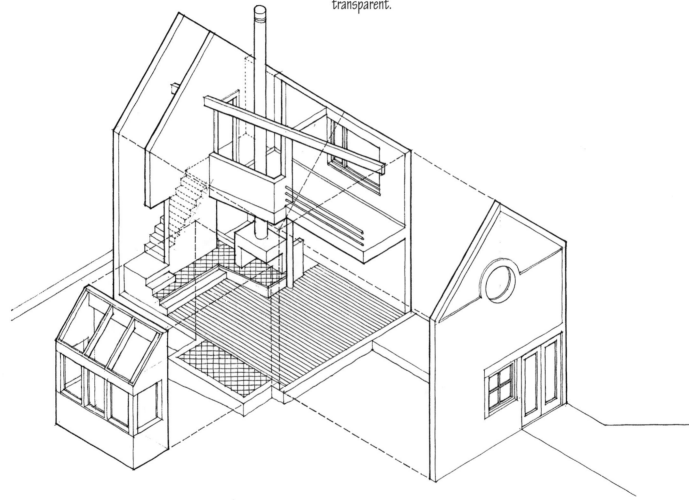

Multistory buildings that utilize repetitive unit plans can be shown effectively by eroding the building form to reveal in sequence the first and subsequent floor levels.

A similar technique can be used to illustrate the plan, interior spaces, and overall form of a building. In this case, a series of paraline drawings is used, each drawing successively building upon the preceding one.

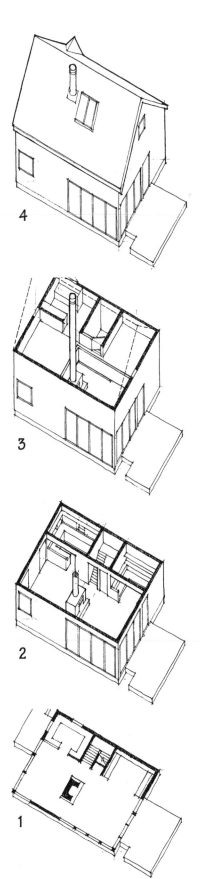

4

3

2

1

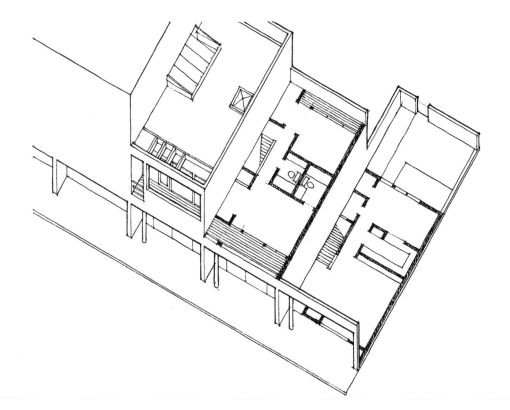

Perspective is the third major type of drawing in architectural graphics. Like a paraline drawing, the perspective is a single-view drawing. Unlike the former, however, a correctly drawn perspective eliminates the optical distortion of lines drawn in parallel and is generally more readily understood, since it, more than any other drawing type, represents the reality of form in three dimensions as we naturally perceive it.

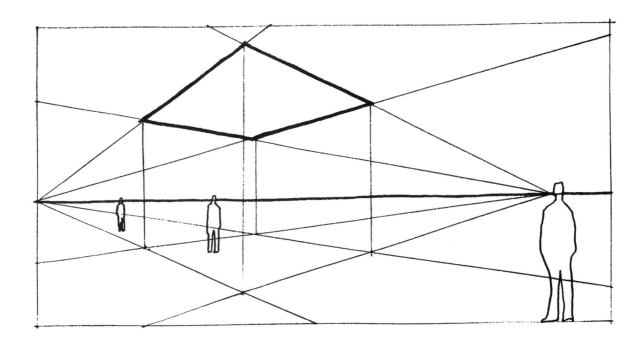

In drawing a perspective, we project on a flat surface the correct oblique aspects of a form as they appear to an observer. In other words, a correctly drawn perspective is the two-dimensional representation of the appearance (i.e., what we see) of an object, as opposed to the reality (i.e., what we know) of that object. The better we understand the form of an object, the easier it is for us to draw it in proper perspective.

Perspective drawings possess four major characteristics, which are utilized to portray a sense of space, depth, and the third dimension within the limits of a two-dimensional drawing:

1. overlapping of forms;

2. foreshortening;

3. convergence of parallel lines; and

4. diminution of size.

(The latter two characteristics distinguish perspective drawings from both orthographic and paraline drawings.)

overlapping of forms

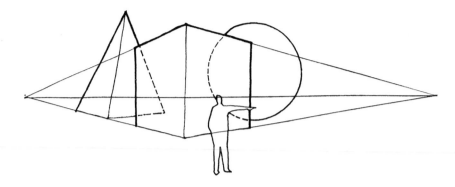

diminution of size

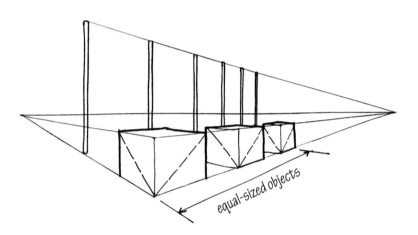

equal-sized objects

foreshortening

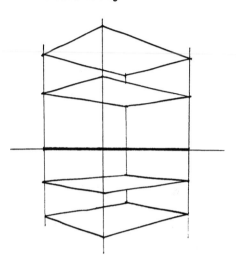

effect of height on horizontal planes of equal area

convergence of parallel lines

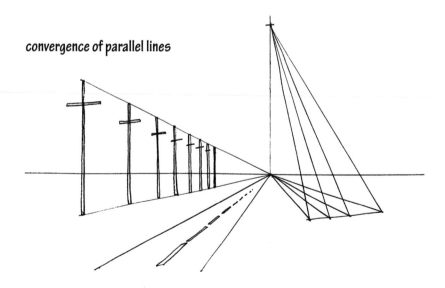

Parallel lines appear to converge toward a common vanishing point as they recede from the observer.

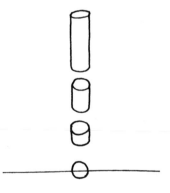

In perspective, lines perpendicular to the observer's line of sight appear to diminish in length as they are rotated away from the observer.

The vanishing point (VP) for any set of parallel lines is the point at
which the sight line from the observer's station point (SP) parallel
to the set intersects the picture plane (PP).

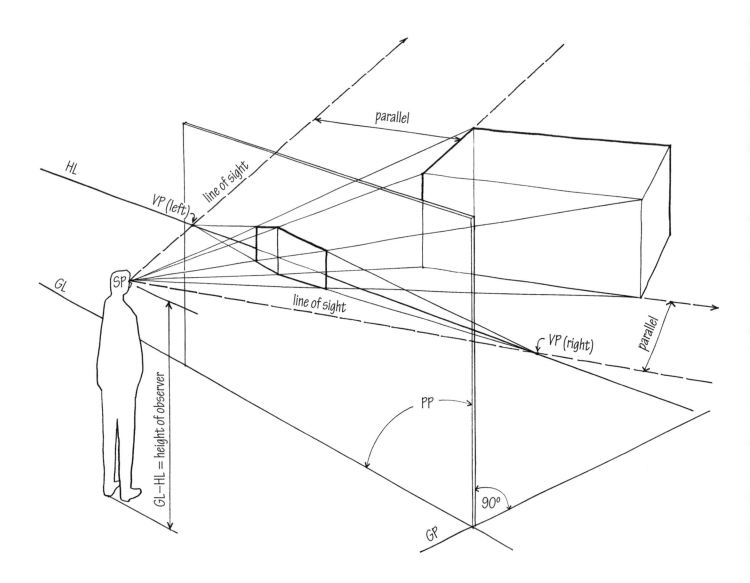

Station point (SP): The position and orientation of the observer. The pictorial effect obtained in a perspective drawing is determined by the position of SP, its distance from what is viewed, and the angle of view.

Center of view (C): The orthographic projection of SP (eye of the observer) onto the picture plane.

Cone of vision: The maximum angle of vision (45°–60°) within which what is viewed is in focus. Everything of importance to be drawn in perspective should be within this cone of vision, since it would otherwise be subject to excessive distortion.

Circles and spherical forms in perspective should fall within a 30° cone of vision if possible.

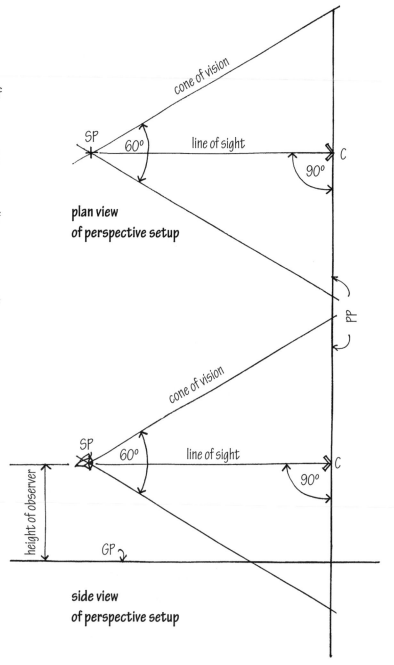

plan view
of perspective setup

side view
of perspective setup

Horizon line (HL): A horizontal line lying within the picture plane (perpendicular to the observer's line of sight) at the same height as the eye of the observer (SP). The center of vision (c), therefore, is always coincidental with the horizon line.

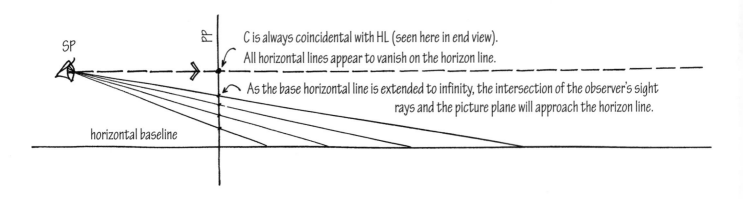

C is always coincidental with HL (seen here in end view).

All horizontal lines appear to vanish on the horizon line.

As the base horizontal line is extended to infinity, the intersection of the observer's sight rays and the picture plane will approach the horizon line.

SP

PP

horizontal baseline

Ground plane (GP): The horizontal reference plane from which vertical measurements are taken. The height of the horizon line (HL) above the ground plane is always equal to the height of the observer (SP) above the ground plane.

Ground line (GL): The intersection of the ground plane and the picture plane. The ground line is used primarily as a measuring line (ML).

Picture plane (PP): The transparent, two-dimensional plane, perpendicular to the observer's line of sight, through which the observer views what is seen in perspective (see page 56). The perspective of any point is always at the point on the picture plane where the observer's line of sight to the point in question pierces the picture plane; in practice, the picture plane is coincidental with the drawing surface upon which the perspective drawing is executed.

Vanishing points (VP):   All sets of parallel lines (not parallel to the picture plane) appear in perspective to converge toward a *common vanishing point.*

Each set of parallel lines has its own vanishing point:

1. All sets of parallel *horizontal* lines appear to converge somewhere on the horizon line.

2. A set of parallel lines sloping downward and away from the observer has its vanishing point *below* the horizon line; conversely, a set of parallel lines rising upward and away from the observer has its vanishing point *above* the horizon line.

3. All lines parallel to the picture do *not* converge but rather retain their true orientation.

SIZE/SHAPE/DIRECTION OF LINES AND PLANES IN PERSPECTIVE:

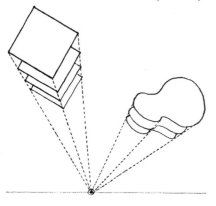

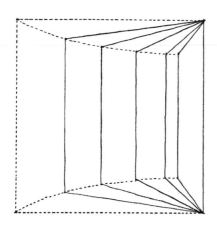

1. All lines lying within the picture plane retain their true length (to scale) and direction. All planes lying within the picture plane retain their true size (to scale), shape, and orientation.

2. All lines parallel to the picture plane retain their true direction but increase in apparent length as they advance in front of it and decrease in apparent length as they recede from it.

    All planes parallel to the picture plane retain their true shape and orientation, but their apparent size likewise increases as they advance in front of it and decreases as they recede from it.

3. All lines and planes not parallel to the picture plane are *never* shown in true size (to scale), shape, or direction.

The observer's *point of view* (angle of view, height, and distance from object and picture plane) is critical in determining the final pictorial effect of the perspective drawing. Pages 60–63 illustrate how the positions of the station point (the observer), the picture plane, and the object with respect to one another affect the final perspective drawing.

1. Height of station point with respect to object

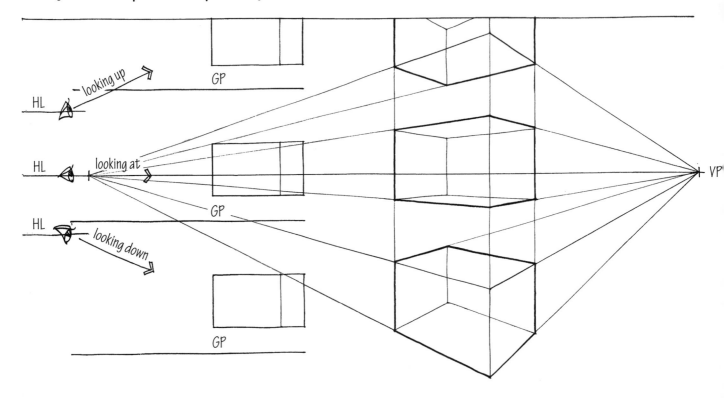

The height of the observer (and therefore the horizon line) with respect to the object viewed determines whether the object is seen from above, below, or within its own height. As the eye of the observer moves up or down, the horizon line and the vanishing points on it move up or down with it.

2. Distance from station point to object

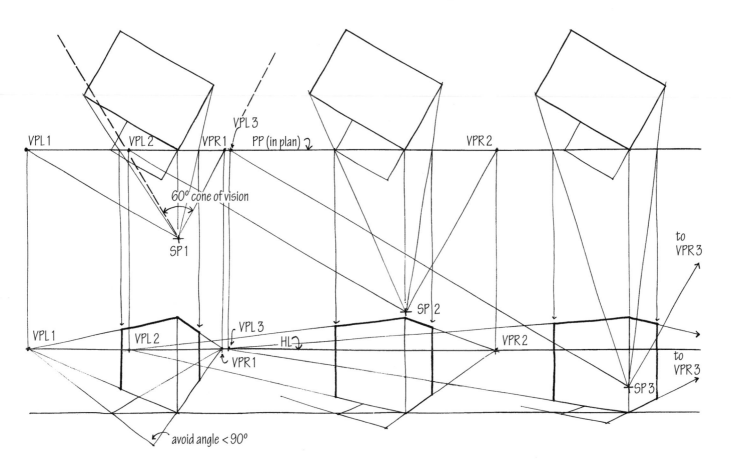

The distance from the station point to the object influences the rate of foreshortening in the final perspective. As the distance from the object increases, the vanishing points move farther apart, the horizontal lines flatten out, and the perspective depth is compressed.

3. Position of the picture plane

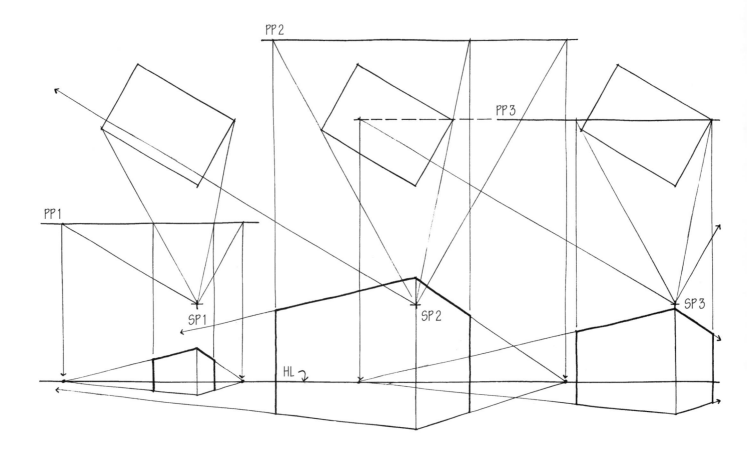

The size of the final perspective image obtained with a given object, a given scale, and a given relationship between station point and object can be varied by changing the position of the picture plane. The nearer the picture plane is to the station point, the smaller the image; the farther the picture plane is from the station point, the larger the image. If all positions of the picture plane are parallel, the resulting perspective images are identical in all respects except size.

4. Angle of view

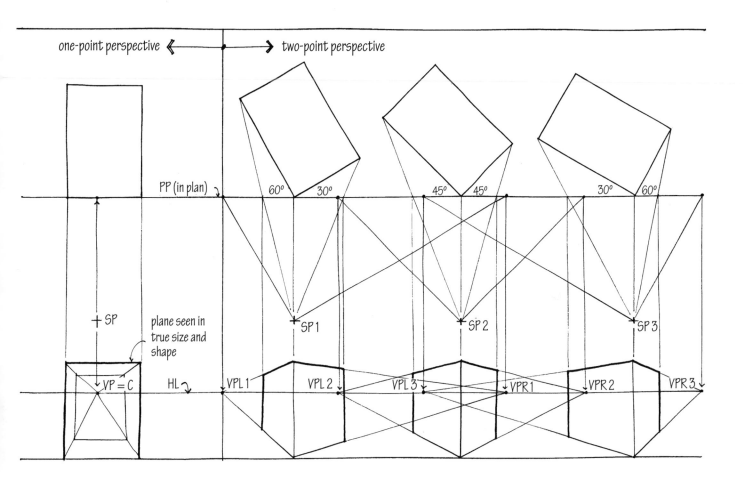

The orientation of the object with respect to the observer's line of sight and the picture plane affects the degree of foreshortening of the various facets of that object. The more frontal a plane is to the picture plane, the less it is foreshortened. Ultimately, when a plane becomes parallel to the picture plane, it is seen in its true shape and orientation.

Depending *solely* on the observer's *point of view* and the orientation of the object viewed, there are three basic types of perspective drawings:

1. One-point perspective occurs when one major set of parallel planes of a cubic form is *parallel* to the picture plane (perpendicular to the observer's line of sight); the vertical (Z-axis) and horizontal (X-axis) lines within these planes remain vertical and horizontal, while the other major set of horizontal lines (Y-axis), being *perpendicular* to the picture plane, vanishes on the horizon line at one point (c).

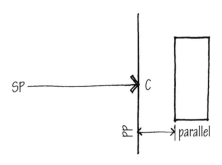

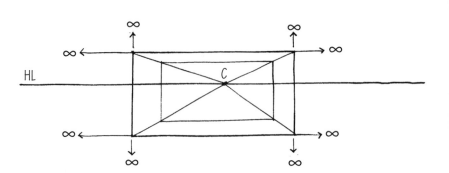

2. Two-point perspective retains the verticality of vertical lines, but both major sets of horizontal lines (X • Y axes) are *oblique* to the picture plane, and both sets have their own vanishing points.

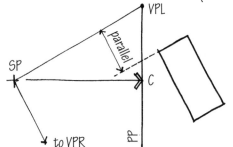

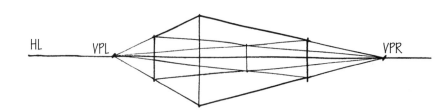

3. Three-point perspective has all three major sets of lines (X • Y • Z axes) oblique to the picture plane and therefore has three major vanishing points.

Regardless of the specific type of perspective, the characteristics, elements, and principles mentioned heretofore remain applicable and relevant. It should be noted that any perspective may have any number of vanishing points. The terminology used in categorizing types of perspectives refers only to *major* vanishing points.

One-point perspectives are useful in portraying interior spaces, some street scenes, and axial arrangements. They are relatively easy to construct but can result in dull and static views.

The following is a method of constructing a space grid in perspective that enables you to lay out a one-point perspective of an interior space.

Before beginning the construction of any perspective, you must first determine your desired point of view: What do you wish to illustrate and why?

1. After you determine the space you are going to illustrate, the station point and the observer's point of view must be fixed in plan.

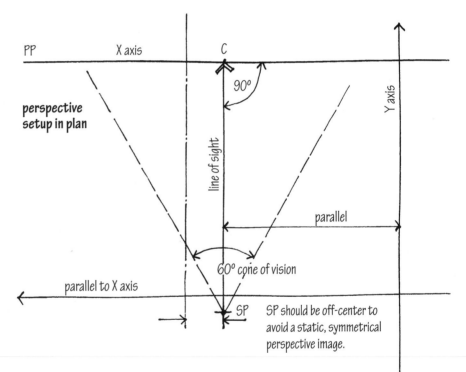

The position of PP relative to SP determines the final size of the perspective image (see page 62); the most advantageous position of PP for ease of construction is coincidental with a major plane perpendicular to the observer's line of sight.

Since this is a one-point perspective, the observers line of sight should be parallel to one major axis of the space and perpendicular to the other.

SP should be far enough back of the space so that the majority of it lies within the cone of vision.

2. Since anything within the picture plane can be drawn to scale (see page 59), draw the overall configuration of the wall plane coincidental with the picture plane at any appropriate scale (the scale of this picture-plane wall does not need to be at the same scale as the plan setup in **1**; it should be selected according to the desired size of the perspective image and the amount of detail you wish to show.

3. At the same scale of the picture-plane wall, draw a horizontal line to represent the horizon line, which is always assumed to be at the same level as the eye of the observer; for interiors, this may be 4' –5', depending on whether emphasis is to be placed on the floor plane or ceiling (see page 60).

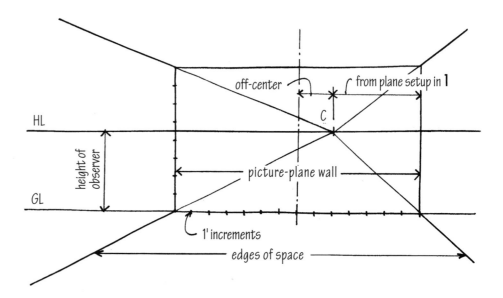

4. Locate the observer's center of vision; its horizontal position along the horizon line relative to the sides of the space can be determined from the plan setup in **1**.

5. Draw lines from the center of vision through the major corners of the picture-plane wall to establish the major edges of the space and begin to define it.

6. Tick off 1' increments along the sides and bottom of the picture-plane wall (this is possible since anything within the picture plane can be scaled).

1' increments are used here as an example; the increments may be increased if it is not necessary to have a very detailed drawing.

7. Through these marks draw lines from the center of vision.

8. From the center of vision measure to scale a distance (left or right) along the horizon line equivalent to the distance from the station point to the center of vision in plan (see **1**); call this point on the horizon line a diagonal point (DP) (left or right); both left and right diagonal points serve the same purpose.

The diagonal point is a vanishing point for 45° lines which cut off equal sides of right triangles, enabling you to scale depth measurements in perspective.

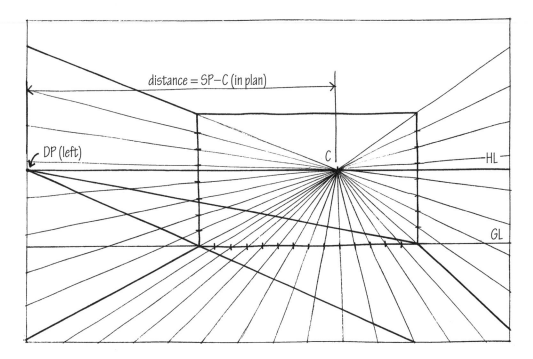

9. From the diagonal point draw a line through the two bottom corners of the picture-plane wall.

10. Where these two lines cut across the 1' lines on the floor plane, vanishing at the center of vision, draw *horizontal* lines.

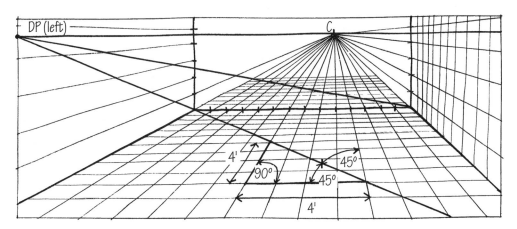

11. You have now established a grid of 1' squares on the floor plane; if you feel there is too much distortion (i.e., if the squares become too exaggerated in depth) in the foreground or along the foreground corners, move the diagonal point further out along the horizon line from the center of vision and repeat **9** and **10**. (Note that if you move the diagonal point further away from the center of vision, you are in effect moving the observer away from the space and increasing the area of the space within the observer's cone of vision.)

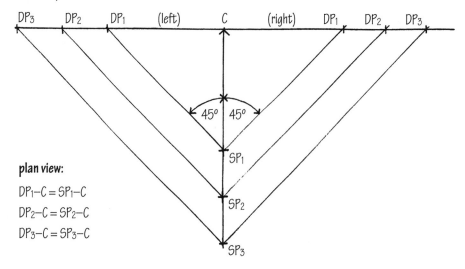

plan view:

$DP_1 - C = SP_1 - C$

$DP_2 - C = SP_2 - C$

$DP_3 - C = SP_3 - C$

12. From where the horizontal lines of the floor grid meet the side walls of the space, draw verticals.

    You have now established a grid of 1' squares along the two side-wall planes and the floor plane of the space being drawn.

With this perspective grid as a base you can lay a piece of tracing paper over it and draw in the major architectural elements of the space. With the same grid you can also locate the positions and relative sizes of other elements within the space, such as light fixtures and furniture.

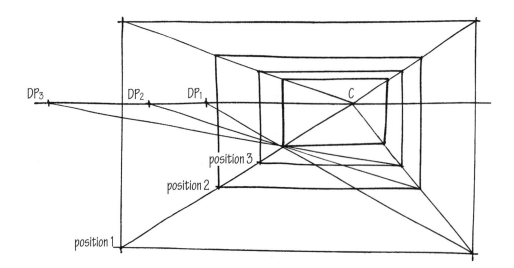

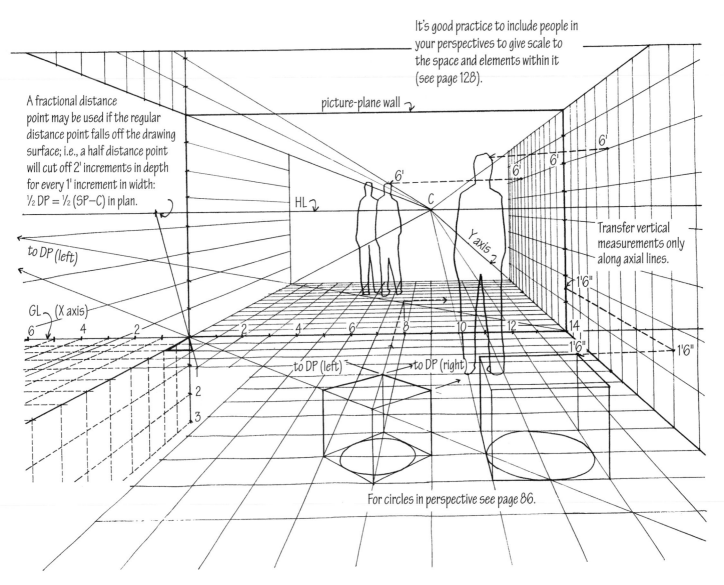

It's good practice to include people in your perspectives to give scale to the space and elements within it (see page 128).

picture-plane wall

A fractional distance point may be used if the regular distance point falls off the drawing surface; i.e., a half distance point will cut off 2' increments in depth for every 1' increment in width: $\frac{1}{2}$ DP = $\frac{1}{2}$ (SP−C) in plan.

HL

6'

6'   6'   6'

6'   6'

C

Y axis   2

to DP (left)

Transfer vertical measurements only along axial lines.

1'6"

GL   (X axis)

6   4   2

2   4   6   8   10   12   14

1'6"

1'6"

2

3

to DP (left)   to DP (right)

For circles in perspective see page 86.

Note that the perspective grid may be expanded up, down, left, and right by extending the side lines of the picture-plane wall and the ground line.

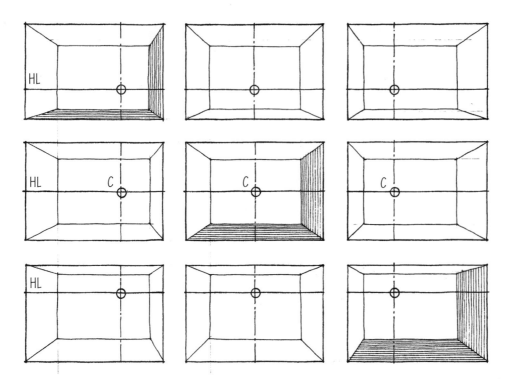

When drawing a one-point perspective of a space, note that the observer's height (the height of the horizon line **HL** above the ground plane **GP**) and the location of the center of vision **C** will determine which planes defining the space will be given emphasis.

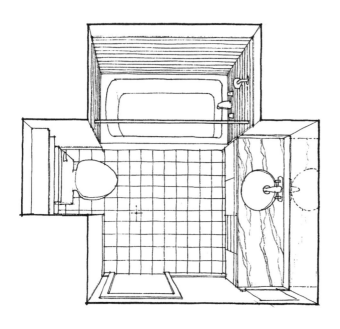

Though not often used, one-point perspective views of interior spaces from above (plan-perspective views) can be effective in illustrating small rooms that contain objects and furnishings of varying heights.

This perspective drawing uses the perspective grid shown on page 69. Note that, particularly in interior views, properly cropped foreground elements can enhance the feeling that one is in the room rather than on the outside looking in. The center of vision **C** is closer to the right-hand wall so that the bending of the space to the left can be visualized. The change in scale between the left-hand shelving and the patio doors beyond, and a similar change between the foreground table and the window seat beyond, serve to emphasize the depth of the perspective.

Two-point perspective is probably the most widely used of the three perspective drawing types. Unlike one-point perspective, a two-point perspective tends to be neither symmetrical nor static and it portrays a more natural view for the observer. It is used for both interior and exterior spaces and forms and is readily adaptable to most situations.

The following is a method of constructing a space grid in two-point perspective, utilizing measuring points (MP).

As with the construction of a one-point perspective, you must first establish the observer's point of view. Determine what you wish to illustrate. Look toward the most significant areas and try to visualize from your plan drawing what will be seen in the foreground, middle ground, and background. Review the previous discussion on the effects of the height of the station point, the distance from the station point to the object, the position of the picture plane, and the observer's angle of view on the final perspective drawing (see pages 60–63).

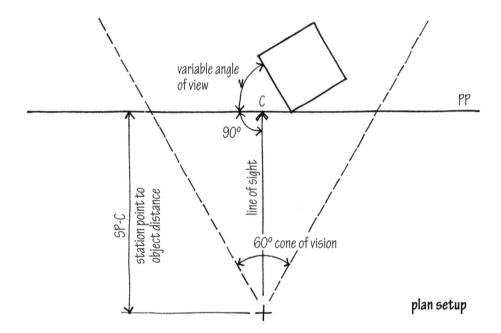

plan setup

1. At a convenient scale in plan:

   • Lay out the major outline of the space or form.
   • Locate the station point, being careful that most of what you wish to illustrate lies within the 60° cone of vision.
   • Locate the picture plane (always perpendicular to the observer's line of sight).

   It is usually convenient to run it through a major vertical element (a corner or a column) so that it can be used as a vertical measuring line.

2. Determine:

- vanishing point left (VPL);
- vanishing point right (VPR);
- measuring point left (MPL);
- measuring point right (MPR); and
- center of vision C.

- The vanishing point for any line is the point at which a line from the station point parallel to the line in question intersects the picture plane.
- In this plan setup, include vanishing points for secondary lines that might be useful in constructing your perspective (i.e., if you have a series of 45° lines in your design, find their vanishing point [VP (45°)] as shown).

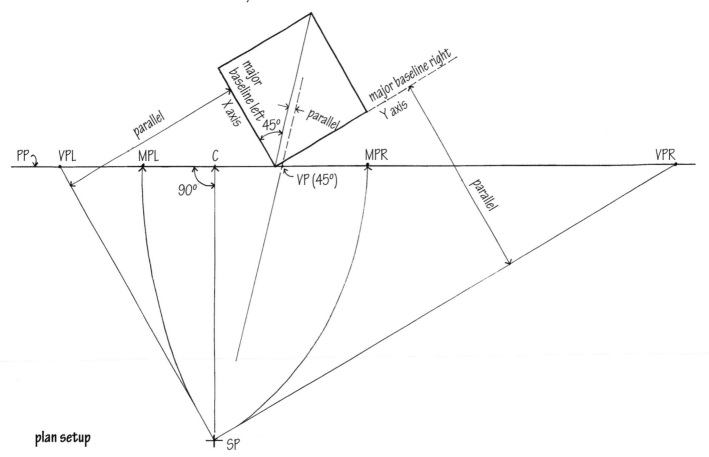

plan setup

- From vanishing point left (VPL) as center, swing the radius of vanishing point left-station point up to the picture plane (this point becomes measuring point right [MPR]); do likewise with vanishing point right (VPR) as center to locate measuring point left (MPL).

3. In perspective and at an appropriate scale (which need not be the same scale as the perspective setup in plan) lay out the horizon line and determine on this line the points previously laid out in plan and wherever the form or space might touch or intersect the picture plane.

4. Where the picture plane cuts across the form or space as determined in the perspective setup in plan, draw a vertical line; this line, since it lies within the picture plane, can be scaled and is therefore called a vertical measuring line (VML).

   Where this vertical meets the ground plane is determined by the height of the eye of the observer; from this point, a horizontal ground line (GL) can be drawn (this line also lies within the picture plane and can also be scaled).

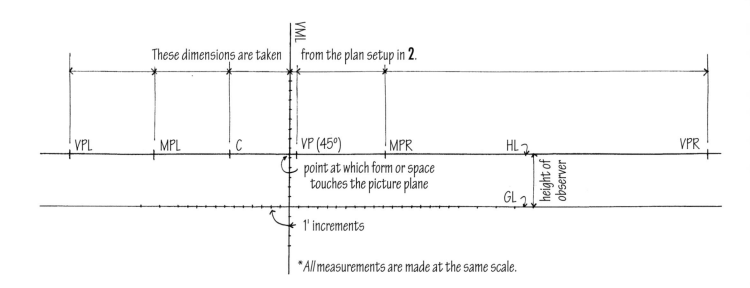

These dimensions are taken from the plan setup in **2**.

VML

VPL   MPL   C   VP (45°)   MPR   HL   VPR

point at which form or space touches the picture plane

height of observer

GL

1' increments

*All measurements are made at the same scale.

5. Scale off 1' measurements along the ground line and the vertical measuring line.

6. From the left and right vanishing points draw lines through the intersection of the ground line and the vertical measuring line.

These are the *major baselines* (X • Y axes) in perspective.

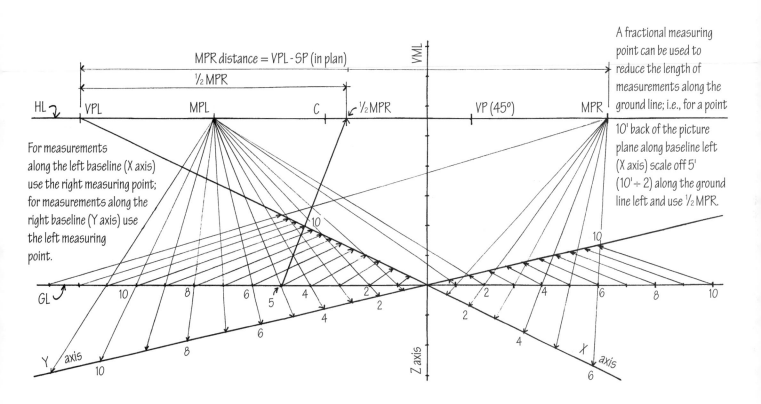

A fractional measuring point can be used to reduce the length of measurements along the ground line; i.e., for a point 10' back of the picture plane along baseline left (X axis) scale off 5' (10' ÷ 2) along the ground line left and use ½ MPR.

For measurements along the left baseline (X axis) use the right measuring point; for measurements along the right baseline (Y axis) use the left measuring point.

7. From the left and right *measuring points* draw lines to the scaled 1' increments along the ground line.

These are construction lines, which are used only to transfer scaled measurements along the ground line to the major baselines in perspective (as you can see, equal measurements in perspective appear to diminish in size as they recede from the observer).

8. From the left and right vanishing points draw grid lines through the *transferred* measurements along the *major baselines* in perspective and the *scaled* measurements along the *vertical measuring line.*

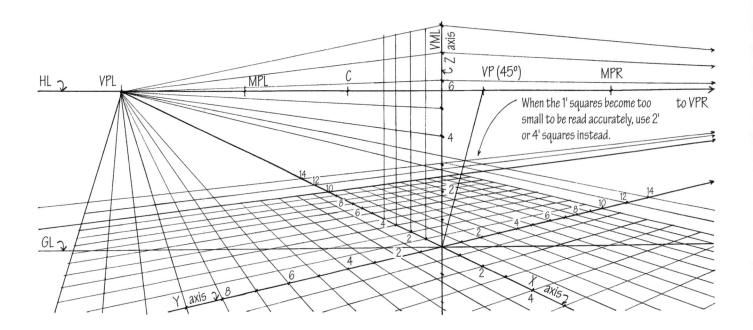

When the 1' squares become too small to be read accurately, use 2' or 4' squares instead.

This perspective grid that you have just constructed is correct for your selected point of view and its specific station point/picture plane/object relationships (see pages 60–63). If an aerial view is desired, for example, then the grid would be constructed with identical relationships of those elements along the horizon line, but the ground line would be lowered to make the distance between the two equal to the height of the observer above the ground plane.

It is good practice to save the perspective grids you construct for possible future use. File them under height of observer and angle of view.

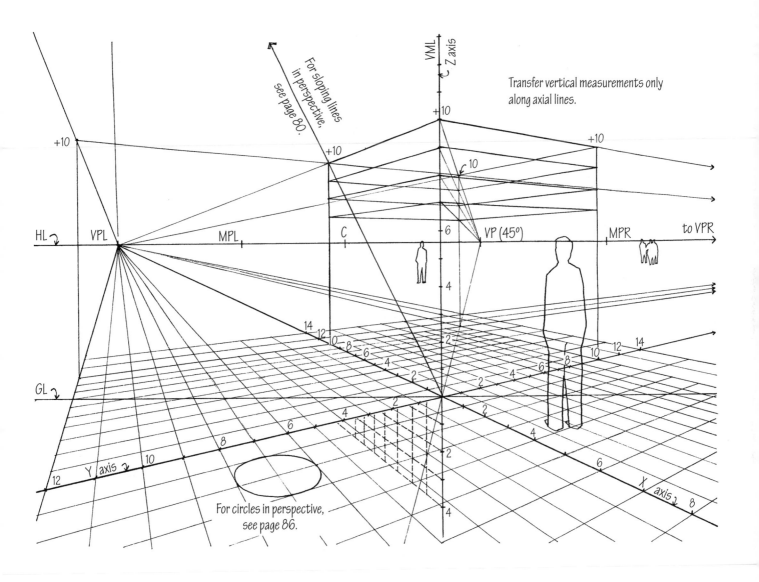

For sloping lines
in perspective,
see page 80.

Transfer vertical measurements only
along axial lines.

VML
Z axis

+10
+10
+10
+10
+10
+10
10

HL
VPL
MPL
C
6
VP (45°)
MPR
to VPR

4

14 12 10 8 6
4
2
2
4
6 8 10 12 14

GL
6
8
4
2
2
2 4 6

Y axis
10
2
2
4

12
8
4
X axis 8

For circles in perspective,
see page 86.

2
4

These three perspectives use the perspective grid shown on the preceding page. In each case, however, the observer's height has been selected to portray a specific point of view, and the scale of the grid has been altered to suit the scale of the structure.

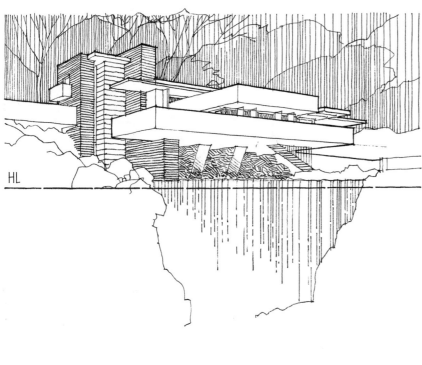

The observer views Frank Lloyd Wright's Kaufmann House, Falling Water, from the stream below the falls.

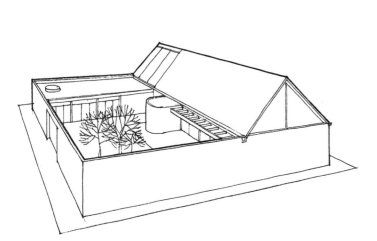

Here, a courtyard house is seen in an aerial view from above.

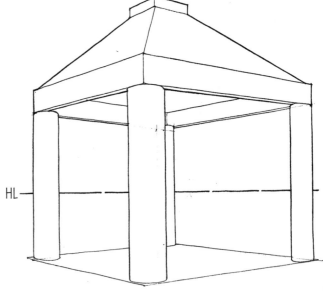

This a normal eye level view—the one to which we are most accustomed.

This interior perspective also uses the grid shown on page 77. Note that the left vanishing point **VPL** lies within the drawing, enabling three sides of the space to be shown and a greater sense of enclosure to be felt. Since it is the left vanishing point that lies within the drawing, greater emphasis is placed on the right-hand side of the space. If the left-hand side of the space is to be emphasized, use a reverse image of the grid.

A sloping line in perspective can be determined by locating its ends in perspective and connecting these points in a manner similar to the drawing of nonaxonometric lines in a paraline drawing (see page 48). If, however, there are series of sloping lines in your design (stairs, ramps, sloping roofs, etc.) it would be useful to find their vanishing points.

*Note that if a set of parallel lines sloping upward at angle ∝ has its vanishing point H distance above the horizon line, a set of parallel lines sloping downward at an equal angle will have its vanishing point an identical distance below the horizon line.

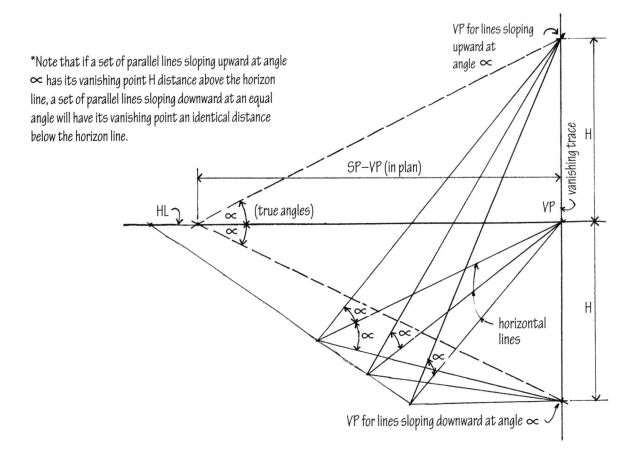

To find the vanishing point for any sloping line:

1. Determine the vanishing point for a *horizontal* line which lies in the same *vertical* plane as the sloping line.

2. A vertical line through this vanishing point is the vanishing trace for the vertical plane.

3. From the vanishing point found in 1 scale off a distance along the horizon line equivalent to the distance from the station point to the vanishing point (from the plan setup).

4. From this point on the horizon line draw a line at the *true* slope of the sloping line.

5. The point at which this sloping line intersects the vanishing trace is the vanishing point for the sloping line and all lines parallel to it.

Another method for finding the vanishing point for a set of parallel sloping lines can be used if determining (SP–VP) is difficult. First, determine a major sloping line in perspective by locating its endpoints.

 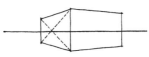 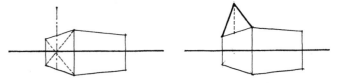

For example, a gable end wall can be drawn in perspective by determining the center of the rectangular wall plane by means of diagonals (see page 83).

Extend the centerline upward to the height of the gable peak. The sloping lines of the gable can then be drawn.

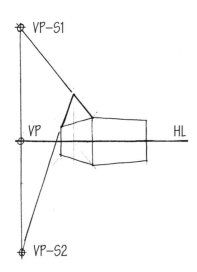

Extend these sloping lines until they intersect a vertical line drawn through the vanishing point for the horizontal lines in the end wall. The intersections mark the vanishing points for the sloping lines and other lines parallel to them.

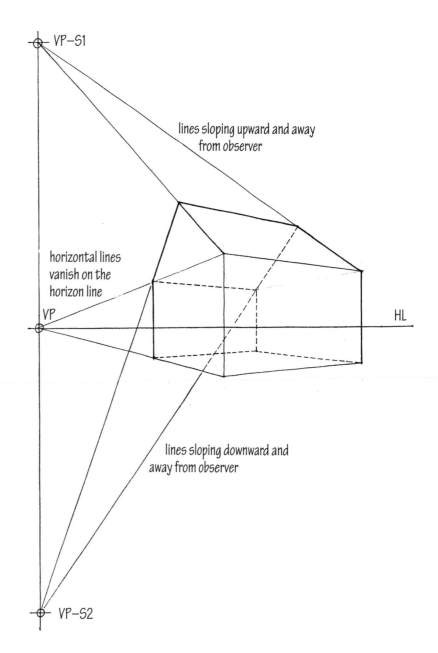

lines sloping upward and away from observer

horizontal lines vanish on the horizon line

lines sloping downward and away from observer

Drawing stairs in perspective is easiest when the vanishing point for the sloping lines that connect the stair nosings can be determined.

1. First lay out the plan of the stair run in perspective. Do not be concerned yet with the individual treads.

2. Extend a vertical plane to the top of the stair landing or next floor.

3. Divide one side of this plane into X number of equal segments where X equals the number of risers in the run.

4. From (VP) extend a line through the first riser mark to determine the height of the first riser in perspective.

5. A sloping line can then be drawn from the top of the first riser to the top of the landing. Extend this sloping line to intersect a vertical line drawn through (VP).

6. Lines can then be drawn from (VP) through the riser markings to meet the sloping line. From these points, the risers and treads can be drawn in perspective as vertical and horizontal planes.

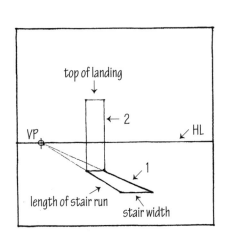

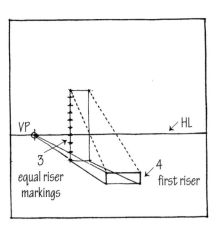

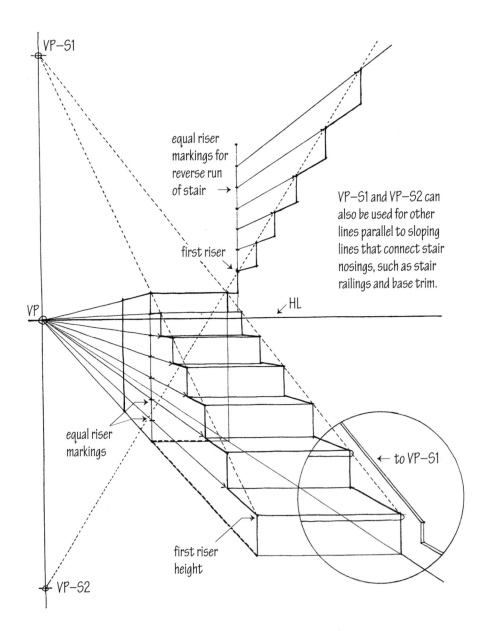

VP–S1 and VP–S2 can also be used for other lines parallel to sloping lines that connect stair nosings, such as stair railings and base trim.

Diagonals can be used to conveniently divide vertical and horizontal rectangular planes in perspective into both equal and unequal segments.

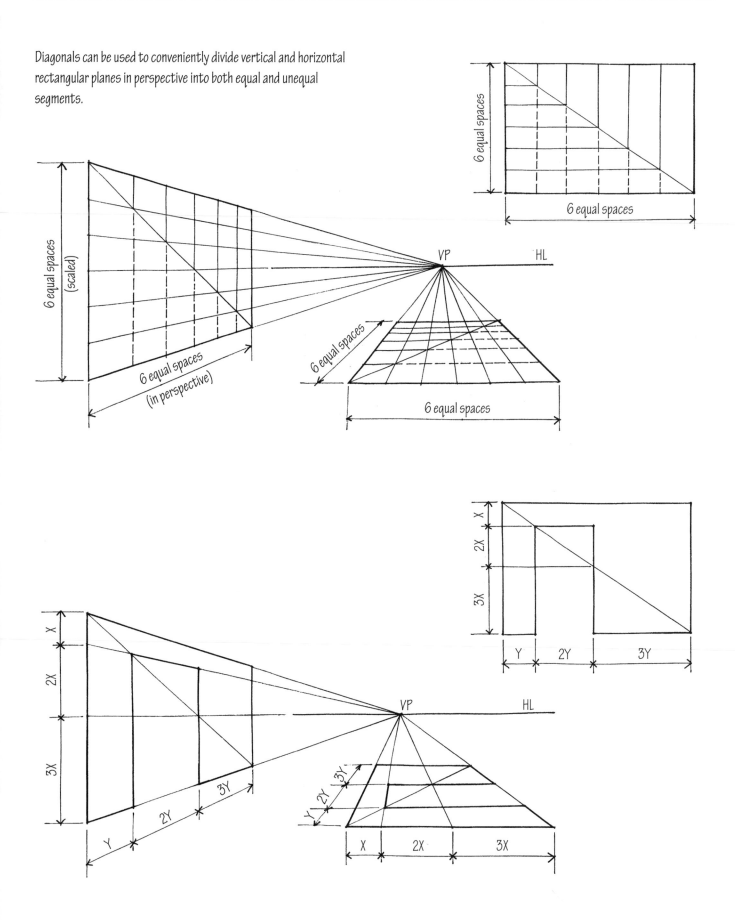

6 equal spaces

6 equal spaces

6 equal spaces (scaled)

6 equal spaces (in perspective)

6 equal spaces

6 equal spaces

VP   HL

X

2X

3X

Y   2Y   3Y

X

2X

3X

Y   2Y   3Y

3Y 2Y Y

X   2X   3X

VP   HL

1. Circles *remain* circles in perspective when they are *parallel* to the picture plane.

2. When the plane of the circle is horizontal and lies at the same height as the observer, the circle appears as a horizontal line; when the plane of the circle is vertical and lies along the observer's line of sight perpendicular to the picture plane, the circle appears as a vertical line.

3. In most other situations a circle appears as an elliptical shape:
   • Draw a square that circumscribes the circle in perspective.
   • Sketch in the circle as an approximate ellipse.

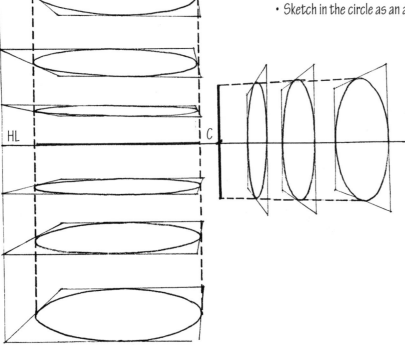

Note difference between diameter of circle in perspective and major axis of ellipse.

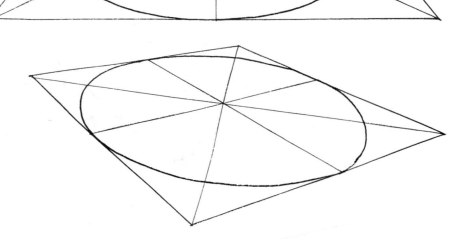

Any reflecting plane surface parallel to one of the three major sets of parallel lines (X • Y • Z axes) continues the perspective system of the object, and the three major sets of lines in the reflection appear in the same perspective as the lines in the object, remaining parallel and converging to corresponding vanishing points.

Oblique lines not parallel to the reflecting surface slant at an equal but opposite angle in the reflection.

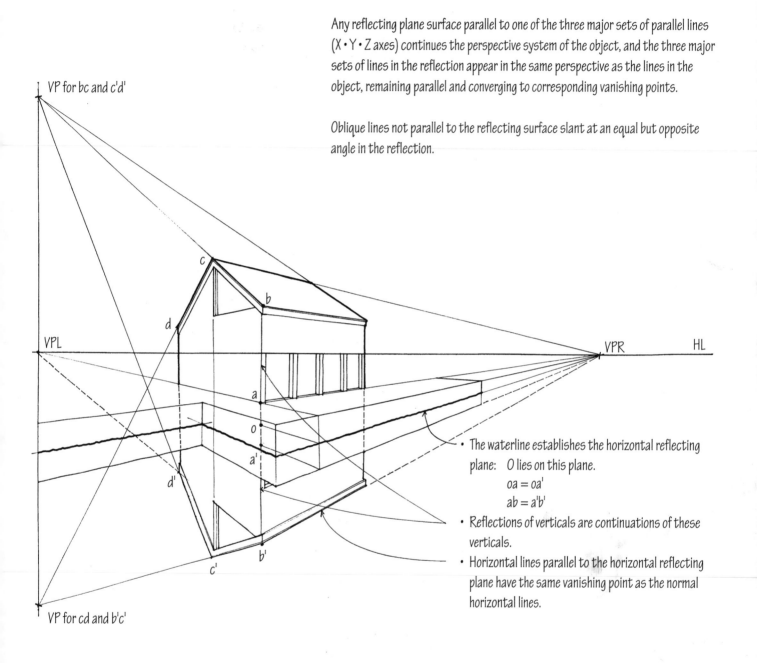

VP for bc and c'd'

VPL

VPR   HL

VP for cd and b'c'

- The waterline establishes the horizontal reflecting plane: O lies on this plane.

$$oa = oa'$$
$$ab = a'b'$$

- Reflections of verticals are continuations of these verticals.
- Horizontal lines parallel to the horizontal reflecting plane have the same vanishing point as the normal horizontal lines.

When drawing a perspective of an interior space with a mirrored surface on one or more of its major planes, the perspective system is extended in a manner similar to that shown on the preceding page. Each reflection doubles the apparent dimension of the space in a direction perpendicular to the mirrored surface.

A reflection of a reflection will quadruple the apparent size of the space.

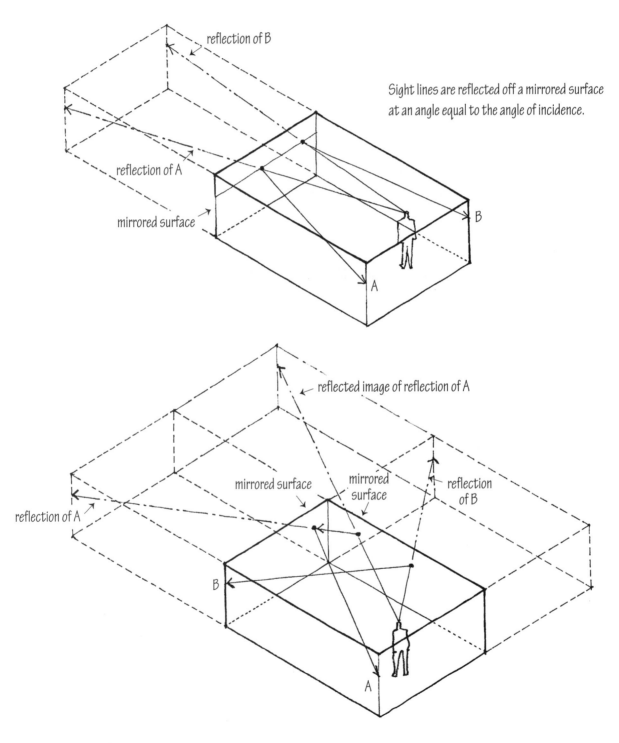

reflection of B

Sight lines are reflected off a mirrored surface at an angle equal to the angle of incidence.

reflection of A

mirrored surface

B

A

reflected image of reflection of A

mirrored surface

mirrored surface

reflection of B

reflection of A

B

A

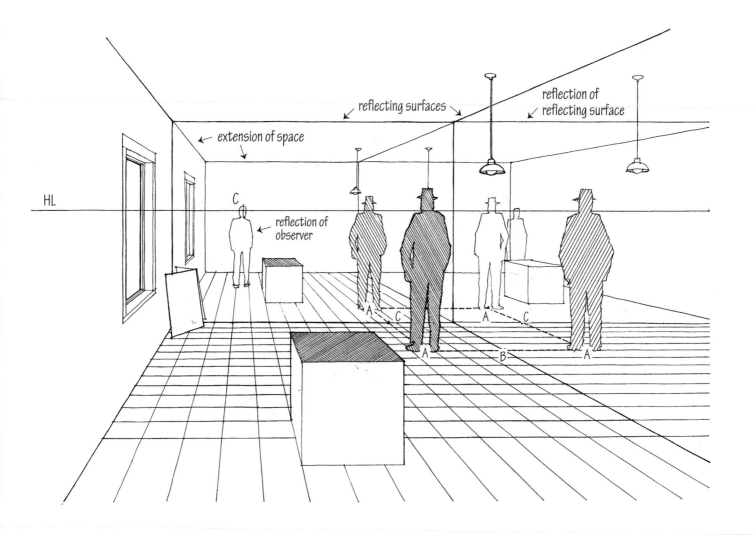

reflecting surfaces

extension of space

reflection of
reflecting surface

HL

C

reflection of
observer

A building section (see pages 34–35) can also be seen in perspective (either one- or two-point), introducing a more natural, pictorial view of the spaces that are cut through while retaining the spatial relationships and definition that a building section normally illustrates.

In constructing a perspective section, the vertical cutting plane of the section becomes the picture plane in perspective.

As with the building section, emphasis should be placed on the interior and exterior spaces that are cut through rather than the construction details within the structure itself.

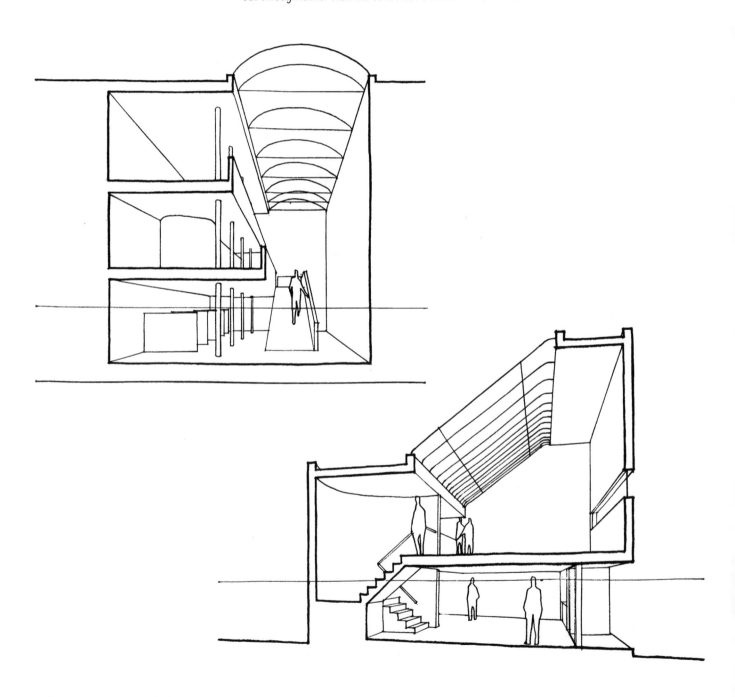

4
Rendition of Value & Context

We derive meaning from a drawing through its figure–ground pattern, its positive and negative images, and the relationship between its light and dark areas.

In the last chapter a pure-line drawing technique was utilized. While contour drawings without value or tone can be quite elegant as two-dimensional graphic objects, they are only abstract images of reality and portray basically an outline world, a world without light.

In a contour drawing nonessentials are eliminated, and only those lines which indicate a change of form are emphasized. (Secondary lines may indicate changes in material.) Since we see an object first as a two-dimensional shape, its profile (outline or edge against space) is its most important aspect, and its profile line should therefore have the most weight.

Plan, section, elevation, and paraline drawings done purely in line are dependent on line quality (clarity, consistency, continuity) and line-weight differentiation and hierarchy to express shape and spatial depth. Perspective line drawings can also use the conventions of overlapping forms, diminution of size, foreshortening, and convergence of parallel lines to portray the third dimension. Generally, however, pure-line drawings convey only limited information and almost always contain ambiguities.

Although all drawing is representational and the difference between a pure-line drawing and a drawing utilizing tone is only one of degree of abstraction, a drawing with tonal value normally conveys more information about the object drawn. Living in a world of light, we find that a *change in tonal value is the basis for our perception of form.*

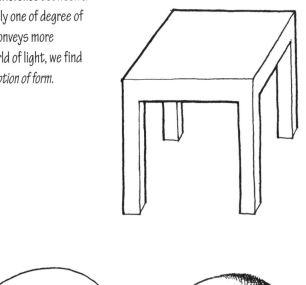

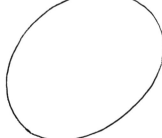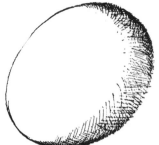

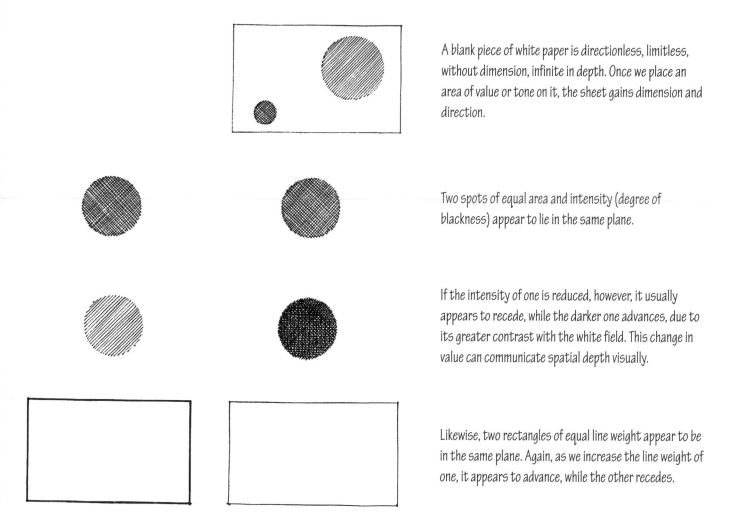

A blank piece of white paper is directionless, limitless, without dimension, infinite in depth. Once we place an area of value or tone on it, the sheet gains dimension and direction.

Two spots of equal area and intensity (degree of blackness) appear to lie in the same plane.

If the intensity of one is reduced, however, it usually appears to recede, while the darker one advances, due to its greater contrast with the white field. This change in value can communicate spatial depth visually.

Likewise, two rectangles of equal line weight appear to be in the same plane. Again, as we increase the line weight of one, it appears to advance, while the other recedes.

If a change in tonal value is the basis for the perception of form, then *contrast* in value is the key to the graphic definition of form. This contrast must be *discernible*. In using tones or material renditions to depict form, you must be able to stand back from a drawing (or use a reducing glass) and judge visually whether or not sufficient contrast exists within the appropriate areas of the drawing to communicate the qualities of form and space you have in mind.

There are four basic techniques of drawing that utilize different media to render form:

1. **Pure-line drawing:**   Careful attention must be paid to line quality (clarity, consistency, continuity) and proper line-weight differentiation and hierarchy.

   • cut lines
   • profile lines (silhouettes)
   • transitions in form (corners)
   • surface textures
   • material changes

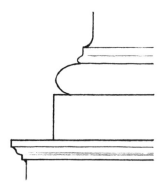

2. **Tone of lines**   Whenever a tonal technique is employed, the discernible changes in

3. **Pure tone**   value (through the rendition of materials, textures, shaded surfaces, and shadows) can by themselves imply the lines which normally define spatial edges and planar corners.

4. **Line and tone**   When changes in value are not rendered discernibly, the spatial edges and planar corners of a form mus t be reinforced by a line technique.

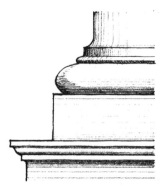

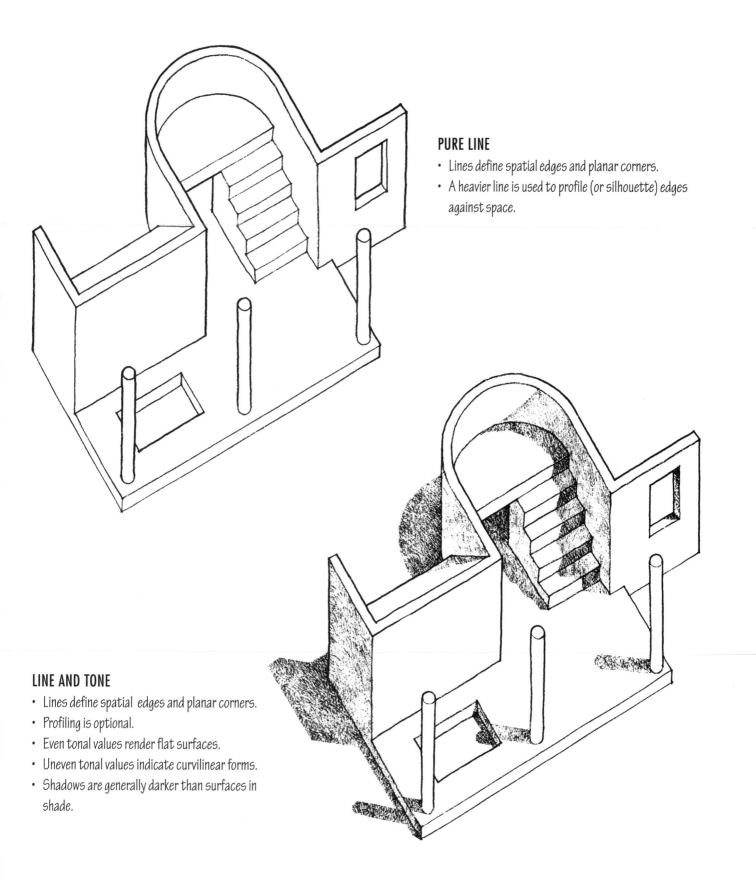

PURE LINE

- Lines define spatial edges and planar corners.
- A heavier line is used to profile (or silhouette) edges against space.

LINE AND TONE

- Lines define spatial edges and planar corners.
- Profiling is optional.
- Even tonal values render flat surfaces.
- Uneven tonal values indicate curvilinear forms.
- Shadows are generally darker than surfaces in shade.

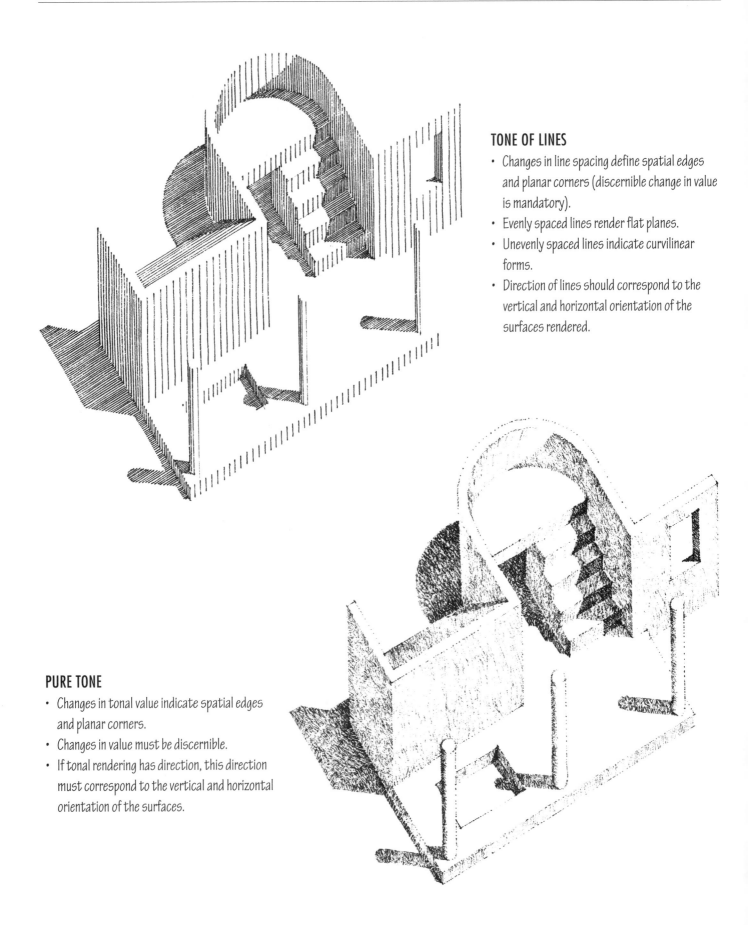

TONE OF LINES

- Changes in line spacing define spatial edges and planar corners (discernible change in value is mandatory).
- Evenly spaced lines render flat planes.
- Unevenly spaced lines indicate curvilinear forms.
- Direction of lines should correspond to the vertical and horizontal orientation of the surfaces rendered.

PURE TONE

- Changes in tonal value indicate spatial edges and planar corners.
- Changes in value must be discernible.
- If tonal rendering has direction, this direction must correspond to the vertical and horizontal orientation of the surfaces.

TECHNIQUE	MEDIA: BLACK AND WHITE		MEDIA: COLOR		PRINTS
Line **Tone of lines**	lead pencil black/gray ink black fiber-tip pen		colored pencil colored ink colored fiber-tip pen		blackline ozalid sepia ozalid Mylar ozalid photostat (negative and positive)
	line	tone	line	tone	
Line and tone	lead pencil	lead pencil	pencil	pencil pastel	Above prints can be used as line-drawing bases for overlays.
	fiber-tip pen	marker	fiber-tip pen	color markers	

	ink	marker
		ink wash
		dry transfer tints
		    and patterns
			ink	color markers
				watercolor wash
				dry transfer tints
				    and patterns
				collage	

Pure tone	lead pencil charcoal ink wash dry transfer tints and patterns air brush		color pencil pastel watercolor wash acrylic dry transfer tints and patterns air brush		

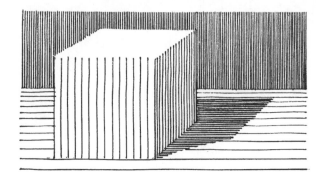

On the facing page are four techniques for giving value and texture to a surface: all four are nondirectional except for lines used only in parallel. When lines are used only in parallel, the direction of those lines should reinforce the direction of the plane for which they are providing a value (i.e., vertical lines for vertical planes/horizontal lines for horizontal planes).

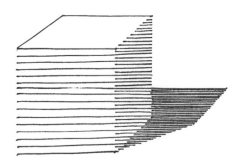

Between white and black exists a whole range of grays. None of the following four illustrations shows a smooth transition from white to black. In all of them, however, at a point between white and black the individual lines, scribbles, or dots lose their singular identity (not their identity as technique) and merge to form a field of gray. At this point there is sufficient contrast with a white field so that a line is not necessary to define the edge of the gray field. This should be remembered in the rendition of shades and shadows to avoid giving too much weight to the edge of a shade or shadow and allowing it to compete with the more important edge of a plane.

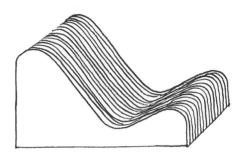

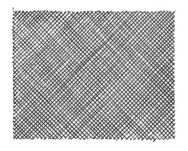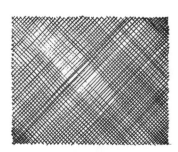

When giving a flat plane a surface value or texture, the rendition should be constant across the entire field of the plane. Lighter spots or subtle changes in value will cause the plane to appear warped.

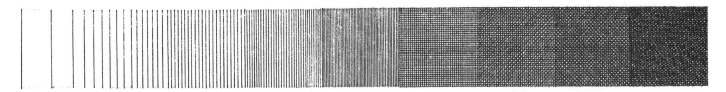

line   In pencil; use an erasing shield to sharpen edge of field when
inking; use removable tape to mask edge field.

scribble   Work against a straightedge instead of masking.

dot   Note that edge of field is composed of a series of dots instead
of a line.

dry transfer tint/pattern

The drawings on this and the following nine pages illustrate how tonal values can be used to enhance the definition of depth and focus in the various types of architectural drawings. See also pages 116–126 for examples of shades and shadows in architectural drawing.

In site plan drawings, the major use of tonal values is to define the building form within its context. The contrast between the building form and the space around it can be achieved by rendering the building as a dark figure against a light field or vice versa (see also page 32).

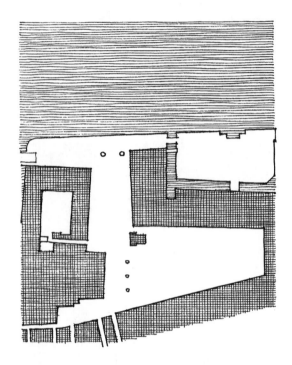

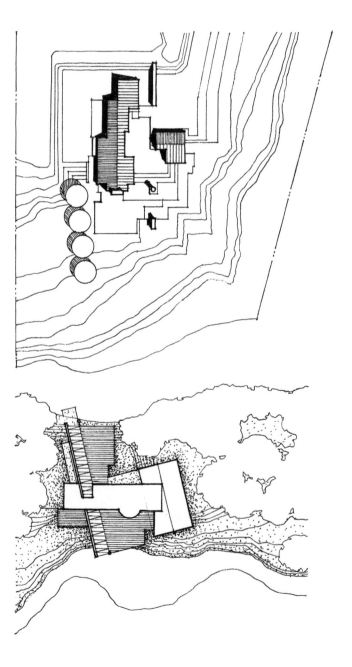

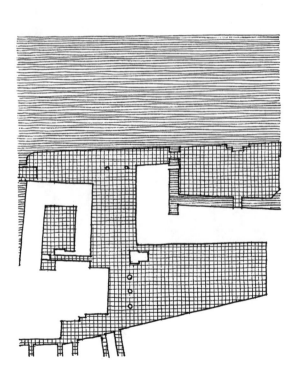

Rendering the floor surface in a plan drawing with a material pattern will give that plane a tonal value. This can effectively isolate and provide a base for elements that are situated above the floor plane. When a plan drawing has several floor levels within its field, varying the intensity of the tonal values can help convey the relative depth of the floor planes below the plan cut. Normally, the lower the floor plane, the darker its value.

If the space defined in a plan is given tonal values along with the surrounding field, the cut elements can be left white or given a very light value. Be sure, however, that there is sufficient contrast to distinguish the cut elements. If necessary, outline the cut elements with a heavy line.

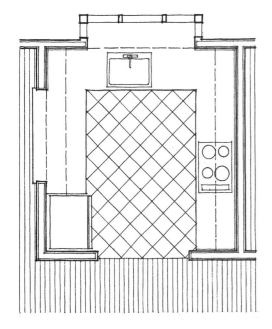

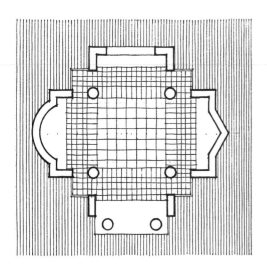

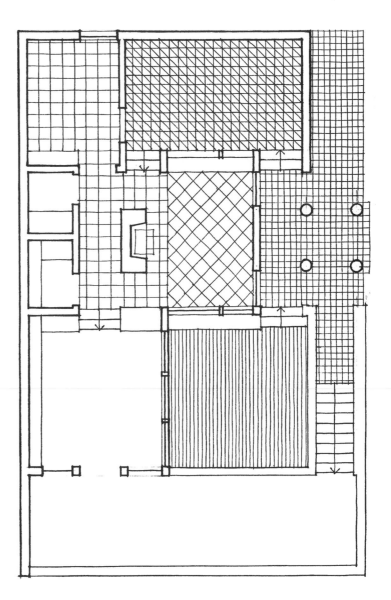

The major use of tonal values in a section drawing is to provide contrast between the cut elements and what is seen in elevation beyond the cut. In the top drawing, a heavy line is used to outline the cut elements. In the center drawing, a dark value is used to bring the cut elements forward. In the bottom drawing, the value system is reversed and the cut elements are seen as light against a dark field. Note that in the latter two cases, the building form's relationship to the earth is clearly indicated by the manner in which the ground is cut and given a value along with the building.

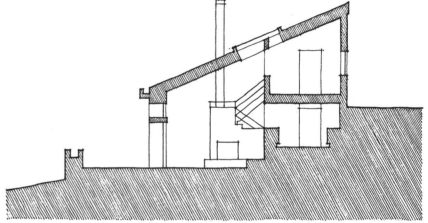

In these elevation drawings, value contrast is again used to make certain elements advance while others recede. The depth of an elevation drawing will usually result from rendering the material and texture of the forward elements more distinctly than the elements to the rear. This value system can also be reversed so that the background is rendered more darkly than the forward forms.

In addition to discernible value contrast, good figural qualities—good shape and closure—are important for forward forms (those closest to the observer) to be seen against their background.

In paraline drawings, the three-dimensional nature of forms and the space they define are more readily apparent than in plan, section, and elevation drawings. The use of tonal values and contrast is therefore used primarily to articulate the different orientation of horizontal and vertical planes. There should be sufficient contrast between horizontal and vertical planes, and generally the horizontal planes are given a darker value than are the vertical planes.

Cuts to reveal the interior spaces of a building can also be indicated by a value.

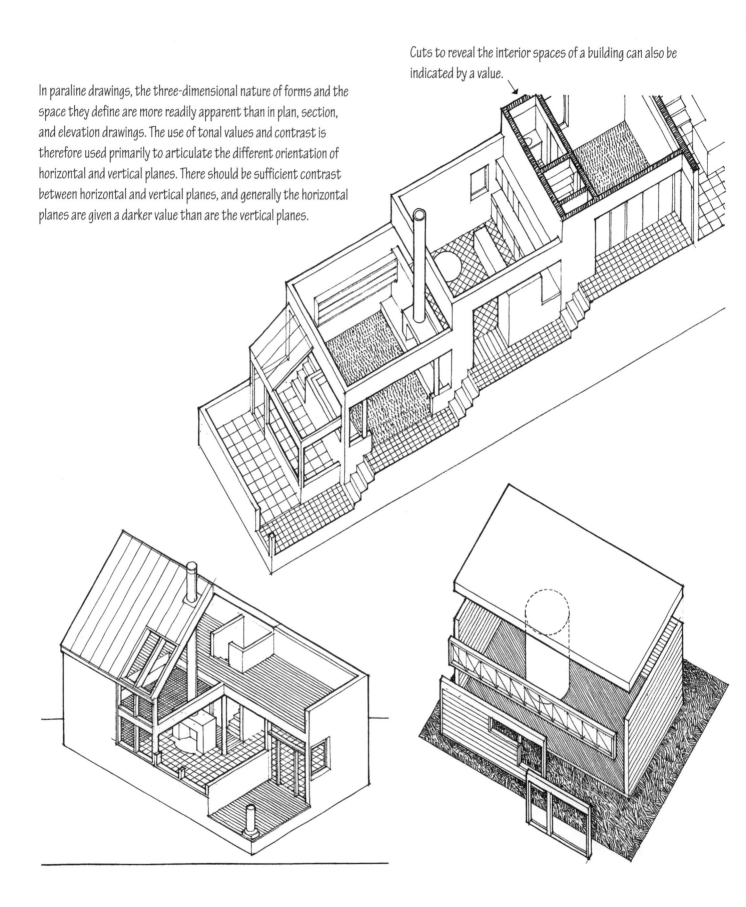

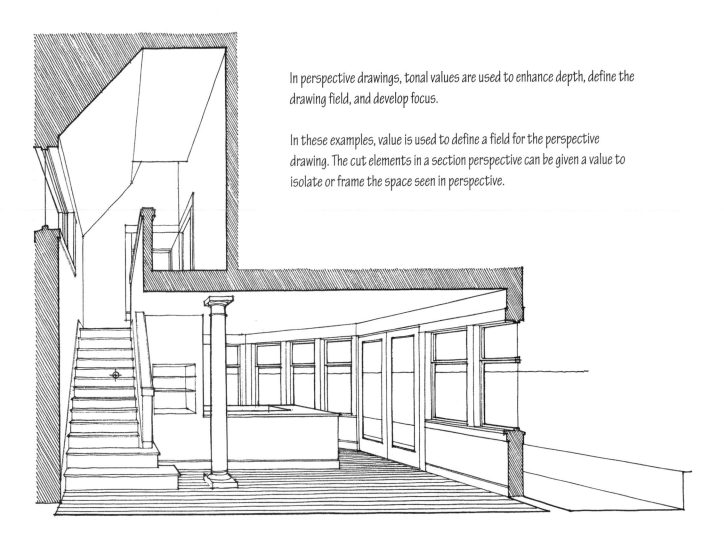

In perspective drawings, tonal values are used to enhance depth, define the drawing field, and develop focus.

In these examples, value is used to define a field for the perspective drawing. The cut elements in a section perspective can be given a value to isolate or frame the space seen in perspective.

Views seen through a window can be similarly framed by a distinct change in value. The scene can be lightly rendered within a dark frame or vice versa.

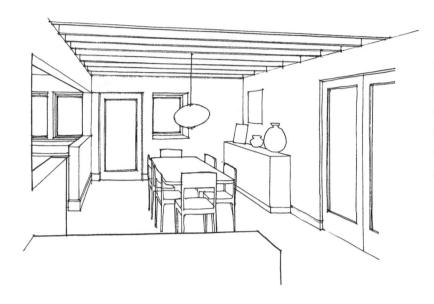

The focus of a perspective can be defined by selectively giving value to certain portions of the scene. The center drawing focuses our attention on the objects within the dining space. In the bottom drawing, the focus is more diffuse since the rendering attempts to portray the quality of light and shade within the space.

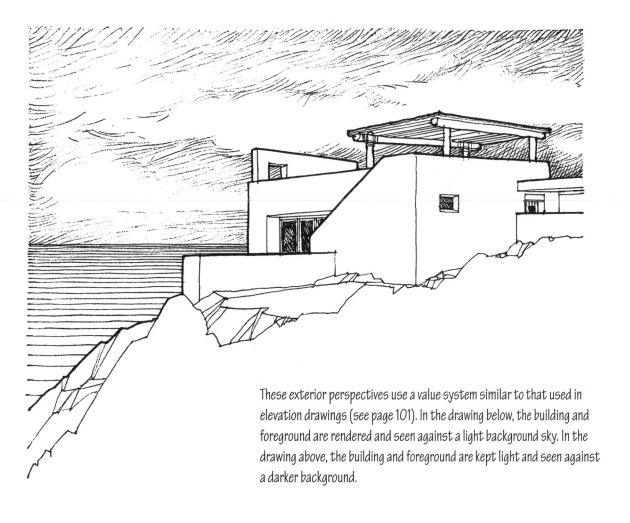

These exterior perspectives use a value system similar to that used in
elevation drawings (see page 101). In the drawing below, the building and
foreground are rendered and seen against a light background sky. In the
drawing above, the building and foreground are kept light and seen against
a darker background.

In this series of sketches, tonal values are used to help frame the views and enhance the depth of the drawings.

In the drawing to the right, the floor and wall elements frame and focus our attention on the figure seen at the end of the space. The figure itself is a dark element seen against a light background. The side wall elements further enhance the depth of the scene by varying in value as they recede.

In this drawing, the focus is clearly on the objects within a space rather than on the space itself.

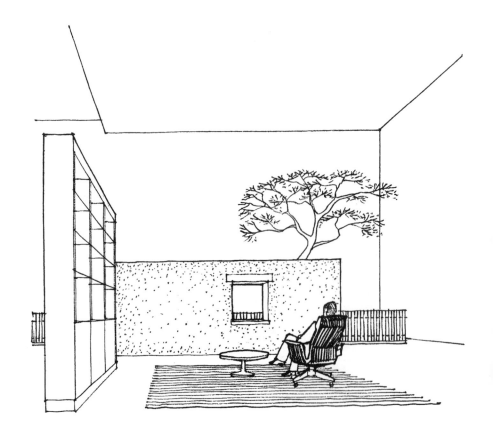

The depth of the space in this drawing is enhanced by contrasting light foreground elements against a continuous dark background wall.

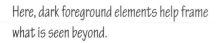

Here, dark foreground elements help frame what is seen beyond.

GLASS

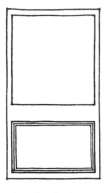 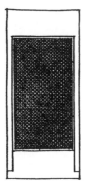   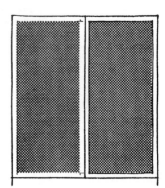

white (outline)　　　crosshatch　　　solid black　　　scribble　　　dry-transfer tints and patterns

CONCRETE

dot (outline)

 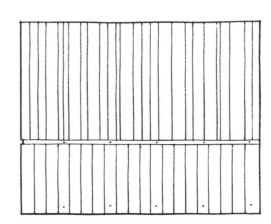

white (outline)　　　　　　board-form concrete

MASONRY

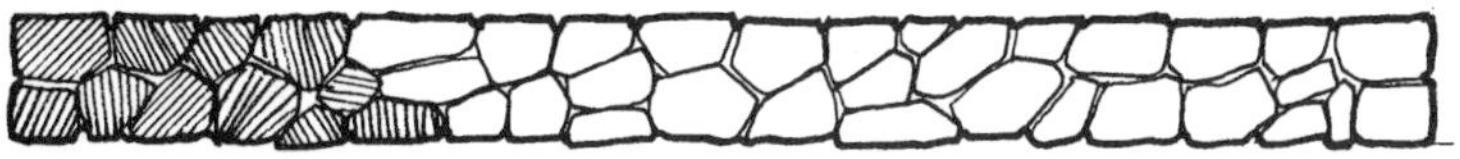

plan

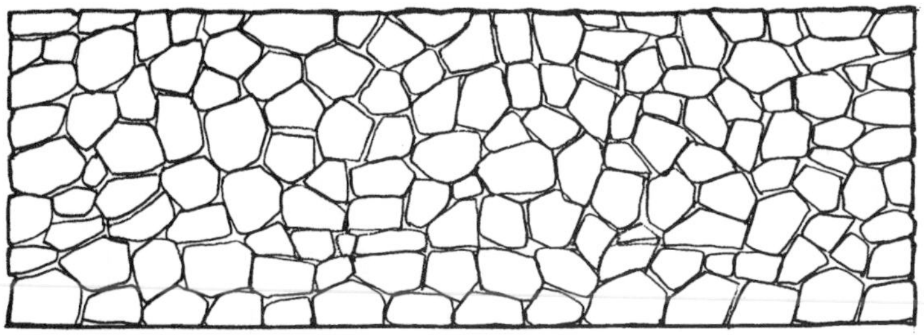

stone

elevation

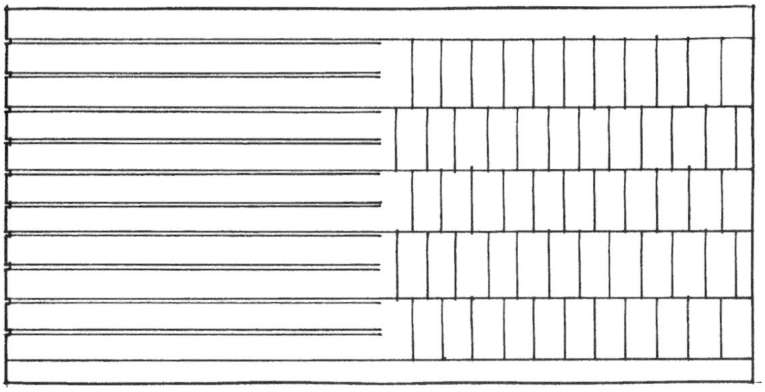

concrete block

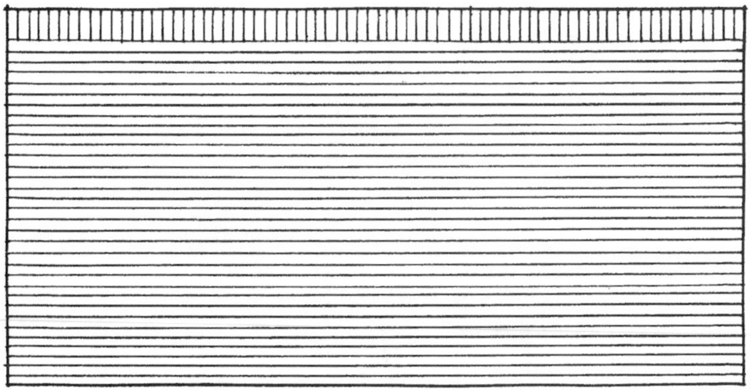

brick

concrete block

WOOD

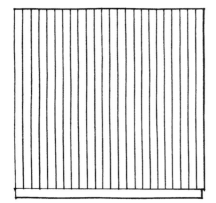

texture one-eleven

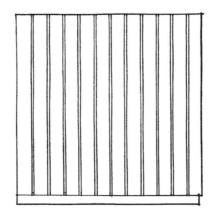

channel groove

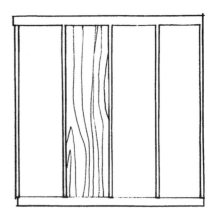

board and batten

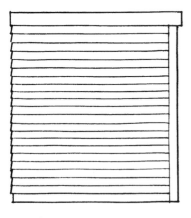

lap siding

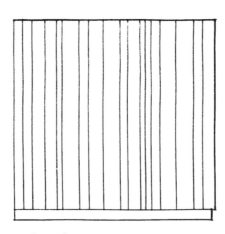

random siding

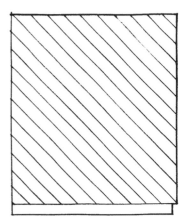

diagonal siding

paneling

ROOFING

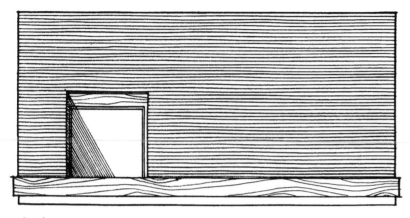

shingles

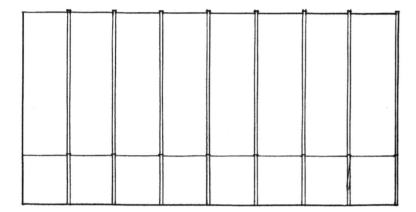

metal standing seam

CONTOURS

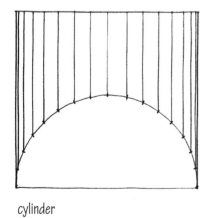

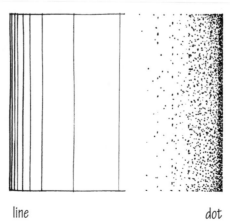

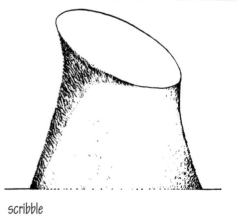

cylinder   line   dot   scribble

Shade and shadows are used in architectural graphics to make drawings more easily understood by expressing both the third dimension of depth and the form of surfaces, whether flat or rounded, slanted or vertical.

The conventional direction of light is the diagonal of a cube from the top-left- (or right-) front corner to the bottom-right- (or left-) rear corner, so in plan and elevation views the direction of light is seen as the diagonal of a square.

This 45º direction of light results in shadows of widths equal to the projections from wall surfaces of vertical and horizontal shade lines.

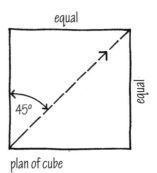

equal

equal

45º

plan of cube

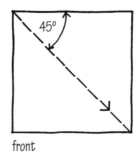

45º

front

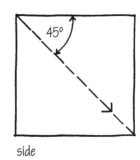

45º

side

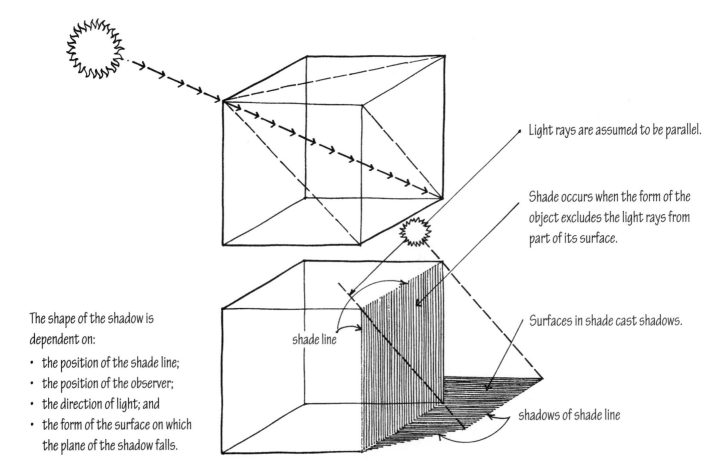

Light rays are assumed to be parallel.

Shade occurs when the form of the object excludes the light rays from part of its surface.

Surfaces in shade cast shadows.

shade line

shadows of shade line

The shape of the shadow is dependent on:

• the position of the shade line;
• the position of the observer;
• the direction of light; and
• the form of the surface on which the plane of the shadow falls.

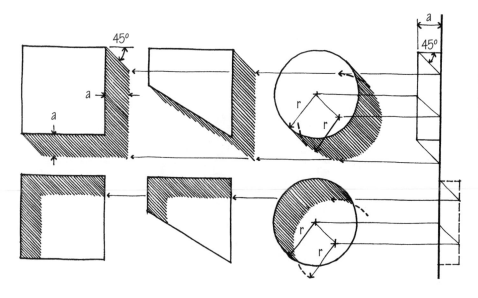

Shadows are parallel to the line making the shadow when the line is parallel to the plane receiving the shadow.

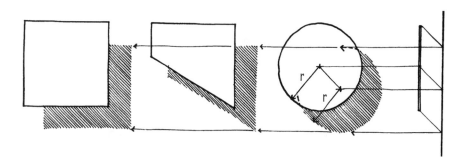

The shadow of any plane figure on a parallel plane is identical in shape, size, and orientation with the figure.

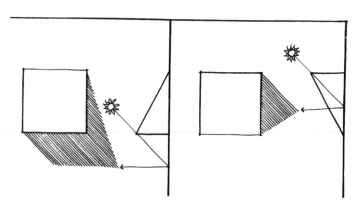

Shadows of parallel lines are parallel when they fall on the same plane or on parallel planes.

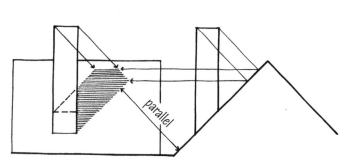

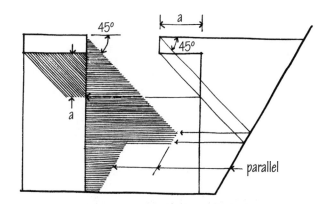

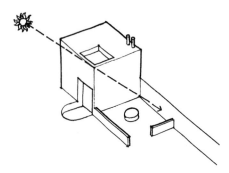

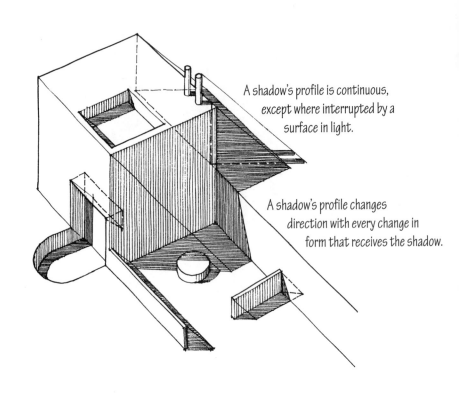

A shadow's profile is continuous, except where interrupted by a surface in light.

A shadow's profile changes direction with every change in form that receives the shadow.

To determine the shadow cast by a complex form:

1. Break down the complex form into its simplest geometric components.
2. Determine the shadows cast by these components.
3. The overall shadow pattern will be a composite of these shadows.

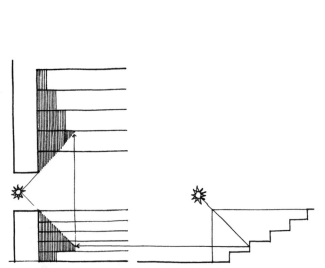

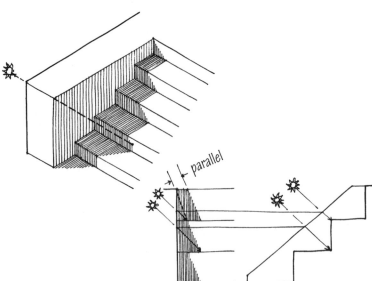

parallel

When the observer looks at the end of a straight line so that it is seen as a point, then the shadow cast by that line appears as a straight line, regardless of the form of the surface receiving the shadow.

The shadow of any straight line on a plane surface can be located by finding the shadows of the ends of that line.

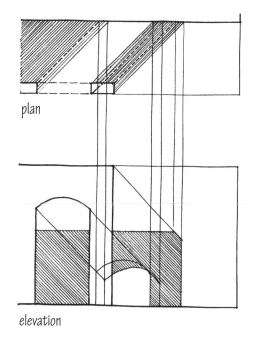

plan

elevation

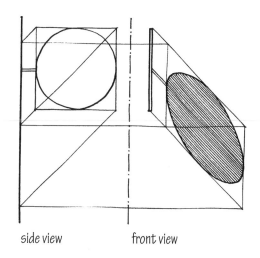

side view   front view

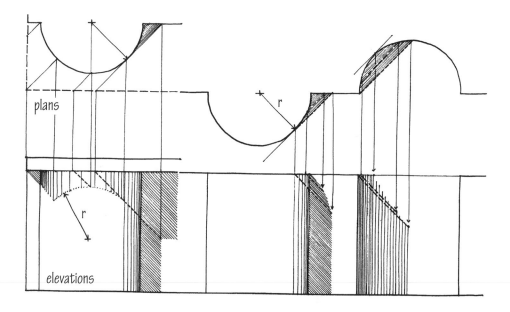

plans

elevations

Shadows of curved lines can be
determined by 45° projections of
critical points (0°, 45°, 90°, 135°).

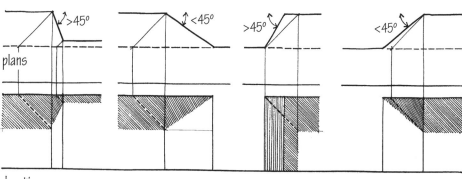

plans

elevations

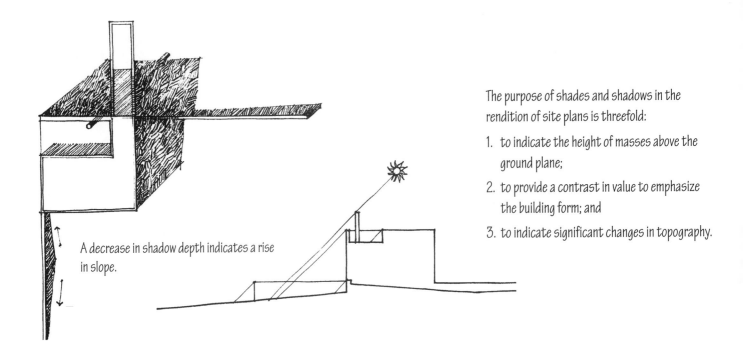

A decrease in shadow depth indicates a rise in slope.

The purpose of shades and shadows in the rendition of site plans is threefold:

1. to indicate the height of masses above the ground plane;

2. to provide a contrast in value to emphasize the building form; and

3. to indicate significant changes in topography.

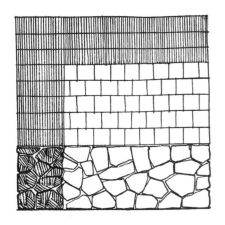

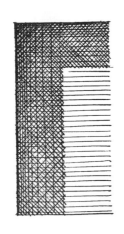

In addition to using a flat or slightly textured (line, dot, or scribble) field of gray to indicate shades and shadows, an alternate method of intensifying a material-rendition pattern can be utilized to indicate the shade and/or shadow without losing a sense of what sort of material is in shade or receiving the shadow.

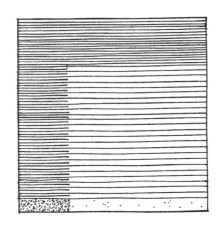

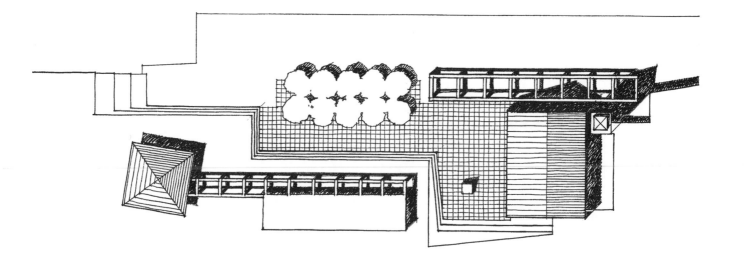

When rendering shade and shadows, note that the sharpest contrast in value should be along the line between the shade or shadow and the adjacent lit surface. Within the area in shade or shadow, there is usually a variation in value due to the reflected light from the lit surfaces surrounding the shadow or shaded area.

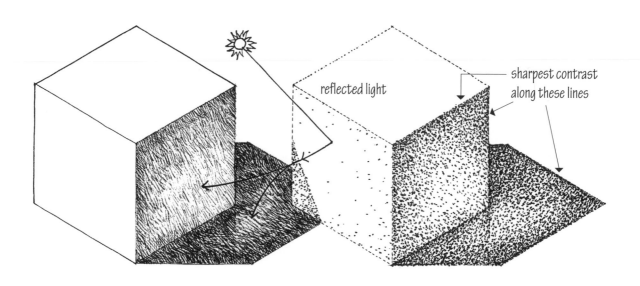

reflected light

sharpest contrast along these lines

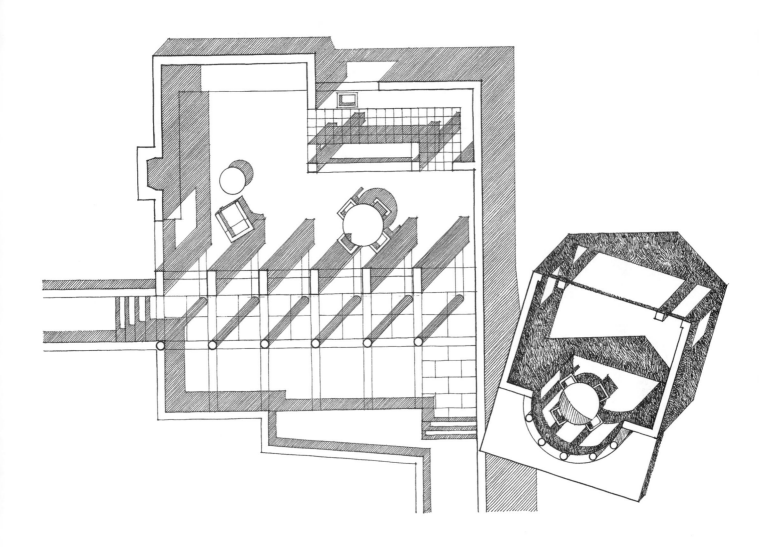

Shadows are used in plan drawings to aid our perception of the depth of the space being portrayed. The intent is not to render the actual condition of sunlight at a specific point in time. The shadows cast by the cut elements and objects within the space merely give us an indication of their height above the floor or ground plane.

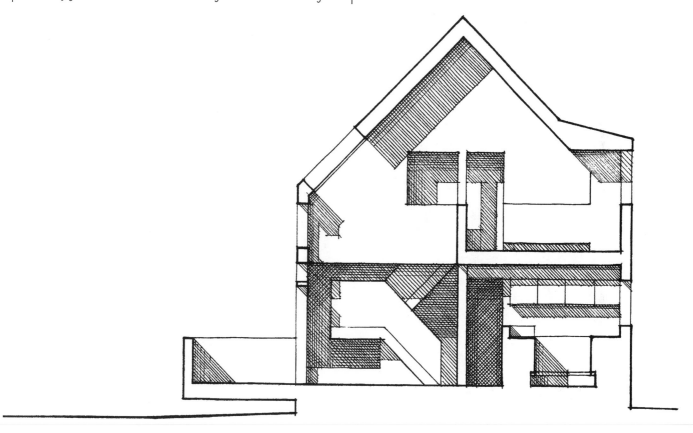

In section drawings, shadows are cast by wall, floor, and roof elements, which are cut, as well as by projecting elements within the space. The depth of the shadows cast by the cut elements depends on how far the cut is in front of planes receiving the shadows.

Shade and shadows are not often used in paraline drawings. However, they can be used effectively if material and texture renderings are not sufficient to distinguish between horizontal and vertical elements and the three-dimensional nature of their form.

The easiest way to construct surfaces in shade and shadows in a paraline drawing is to have the light rays striking the form come from either the observer's right or left. The plane defined by the actual and bearing direction of sunlight is assumed to be perpendicular to the observer's line of sight. Thus a 45° ray will always appear as a 45° line in the drawing. Shadows cast by vertical elements can then be easily constructed using a 45° triangle. Shadows of more complex forms can be built up from shadows cast by vertical lines in the forms.

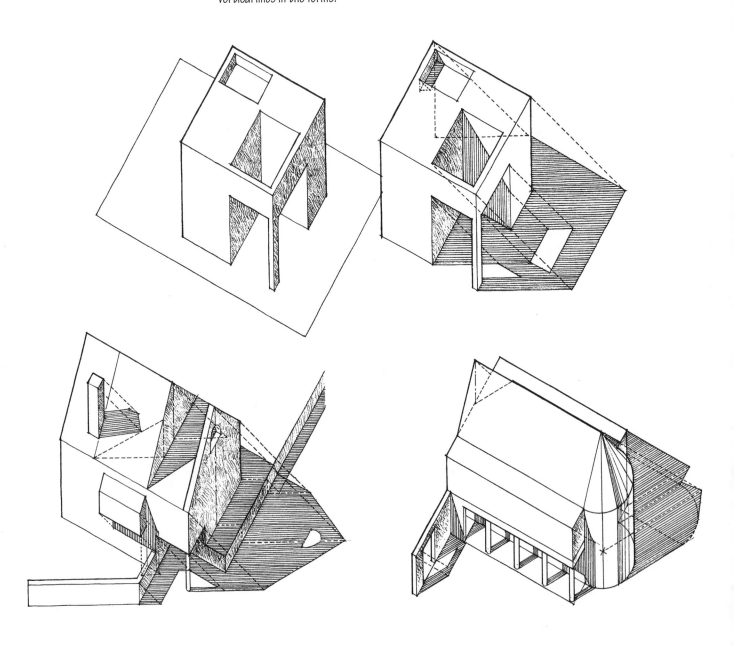

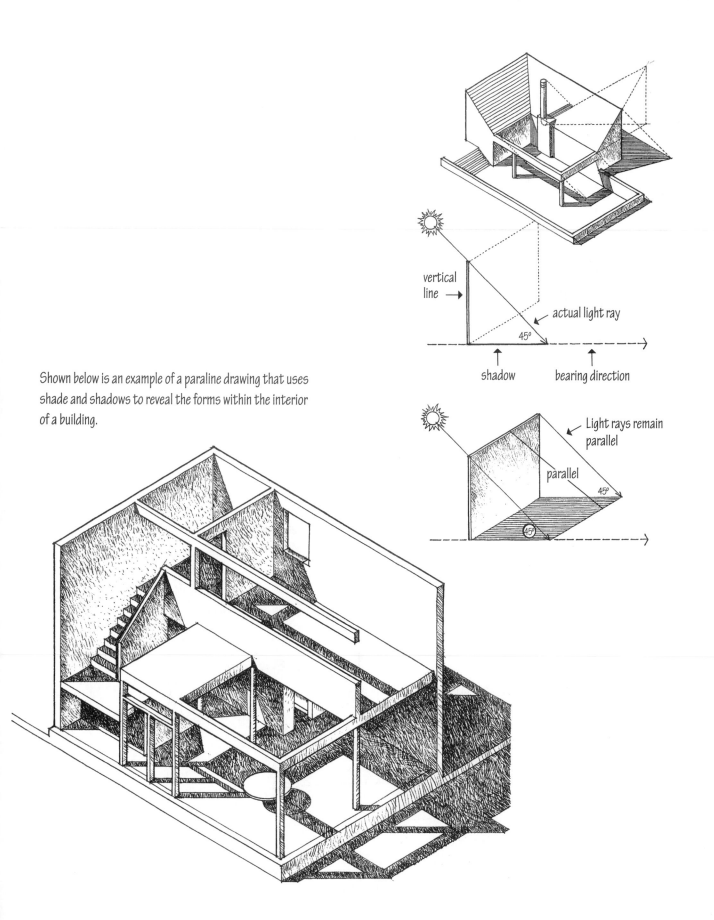

Shown below is an example of a paraline drawing that uses shade and shadows to reveal the forms within the interior of a building.

vertical line →

actual light ray

45°

shadow ↑   ↑ bearing direction

Light rays remain parallel

parallel

45°

45°

Shade and shadows in perspective drawings require the use of sloping lines to represent the actual light rays. The vanishing point for the bearing direction of the light rays—a horizontal line—must first be determined along the horizon line. For light rays coming from behind the observer, the vanishing point for the actual light rays will be directly below the vanishing point for their bearing direction (VP–BD). To determine the vanishing point for the light rays (VP–LR), construct one 45° triangle in perspective and extend the hypotenuse down until it intersects a vertical line from (VP–BD). All other light rays will converge at this same point.

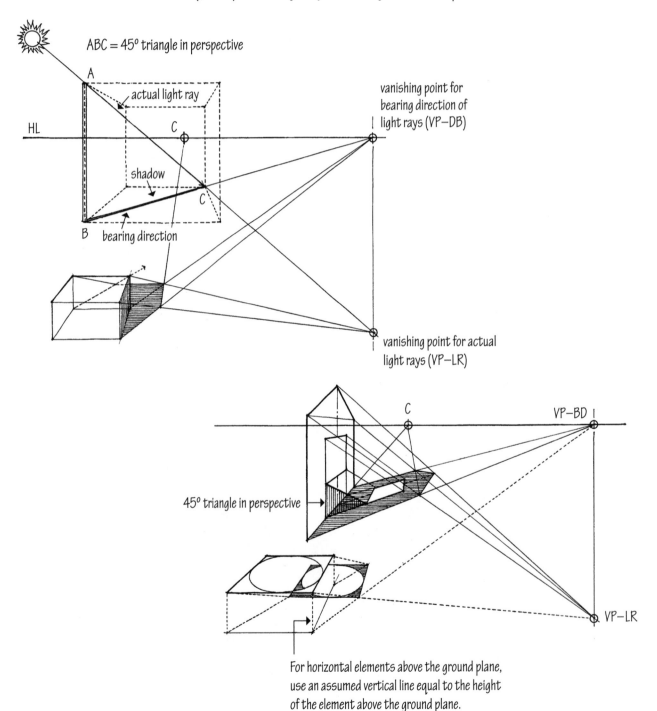

ABC = 45° triangle in perspective

actual light ray

C

HL

shadow

C

B   bearing direction

vanishing point for
bearing direction of
light rays (VP–DB)

vanishing point for actual
light rays (VP–LR)

C

VP–BD

45° triangle in perspective

VP–LR

For horizontal elements above the ground plane,
use an assumed vertical line equal to the height
of the element above the ground plane.

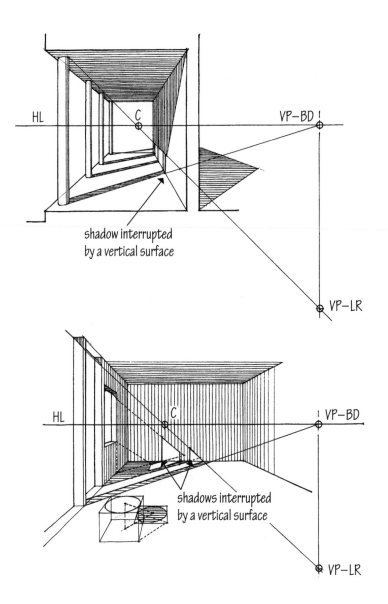

Where a vertical or sloping plane interrupts a shadow on a horizontal plane, imagine that a 45° triangle slices through the interrupting surface. The intersection represents the continuation of the shadow line.

shadow interrupted by a vertical surface

shadows interrupted by a vertical surface

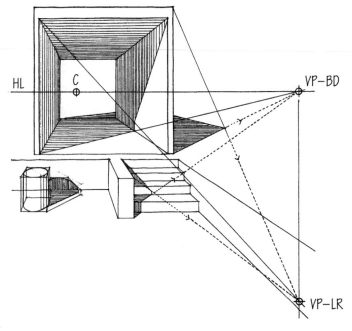

In two-point perspective, the simplest way to cast shaded surfaces and shadows is to assume that the bearing direction for the light rays comes from either the observer's right or left and is parallel to the picture plane and perpendicular to the observer's line of sight. 45° triangles can then be used to determine the actual light rays and the shadows cast by vertical elements in perspective. The light rays, parallel to the picture plane, remain at a 45° angle to the ground plane.

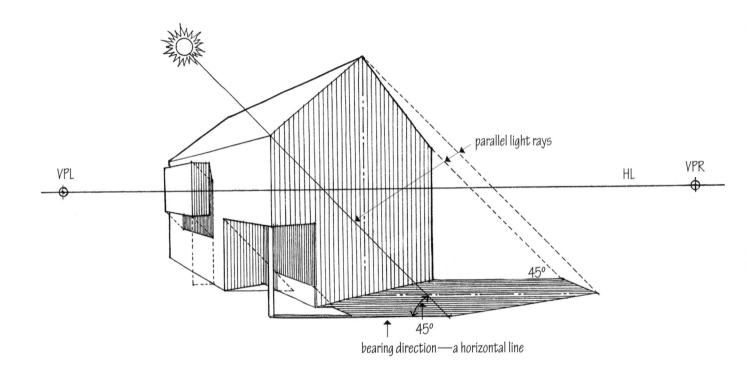

parallel light rays

VPL

HL

VPR

45°

45°

bearing direction—a horizontal line

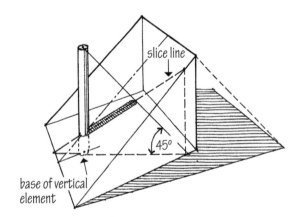

slice line

45°

base of vertical
element

To determine how a shadow is cast by a vertical element onto a sloping surface, extend the vertical element down to the base of the sloping surface. Construct a 45° triangle with the vertical element as one of the triangle's sides. Slice the sloping surface along the plane of the triangle. The shadow falls along this slice line and terminates at the hypotenuse of the 45° triangle.

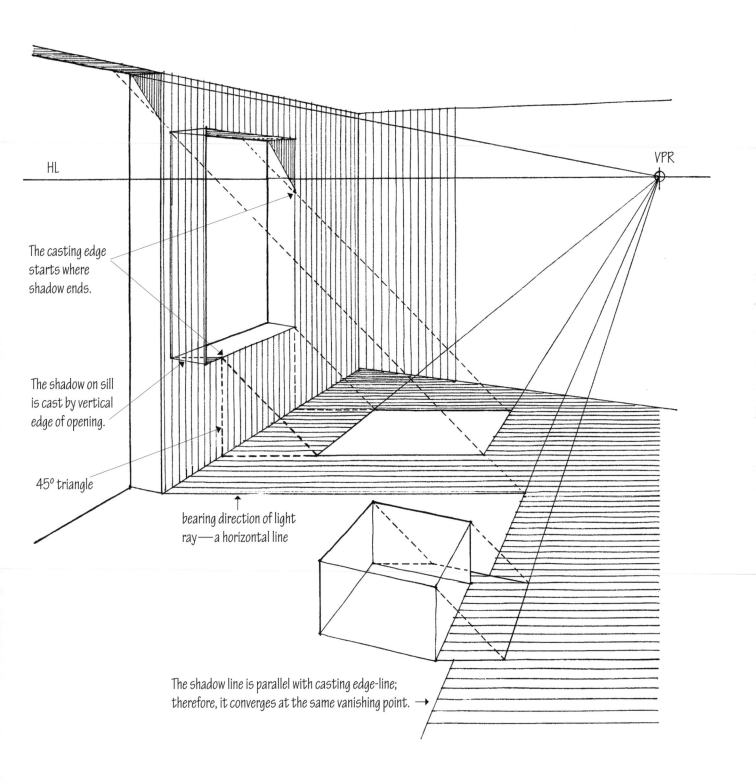

HL

The casting edge
starts where
shadow ends.

The shadow on sill
is cast by vertical
edge of opening.

45° triangle

bearing direction of light
ray—a horizontal line

VPR

The shadow line is parallel with casting edge-line;
therefore, it converges at the same vanishing point. →

Shadows cast by light rays not parallel to the picture plane are constructed in a manner similar to that used in one-point perspective. First, the vanishing point for the bearing direction of the light rays (VP–BD) is located on the horizon line. Then an actual light ray is extended to intersect a vertical line drawn from VP–BD. This intersection (VP–LR) is the vanishing point for all actual light rays.

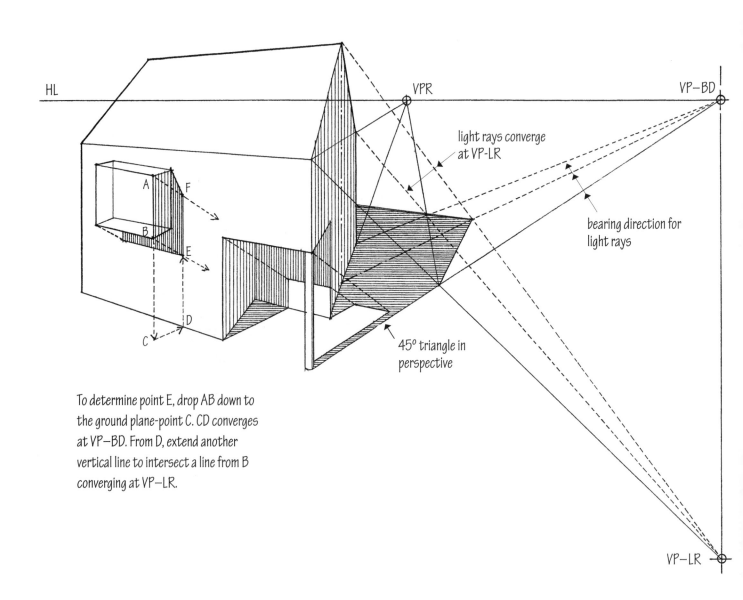

HL

VPR

VP–BD

light rays converge
at VP-LR

bearing direction for
light rays

A
F
B
E
D
C

45° triangle in
perspective

VP–LR

To determine point E, drop AB down to the ground plane-point C. CD converges at VP–BD. From D, extend another vertical line to intersect a line from B converging at VP–LR.

In the discussion of the three major types of architectural drawing in Chapter 3, you were encouraged to illustrate architecture in its context. This inclusion of the physical environs was done primarily by extending the ground line or plane and indicating the adjacent form, whether natural topography or construction. The importance of providing context in architectural drawings lies in the need to design and evaluate architecture in relationship to its environment, whether urban or rural, old or new.

The purpose of this section is to enable you to indicate as clearly as possible, without obscuring the focus on architecture, not only the physical but also the human context, and in so doing to indicate also the scale and use of the spaced depicted.

The following contextual devices will be illustrated:
- People
- Furniture
- Cars
- Landscaping

In order not to obscure the purpose of an architectural drawing:

1. Use only those contextual devices necessary to communicate context, scale, and usage.

2. Draw contextual devices simply, with a minimum of detail.

3. Never obscure structural and space-defining elements and their relationships.

4. The size, weight (value), and placement of contextual devices must be seen as important elements in a drawing's overall composition.

The viewer of a drawing relates to the human figures within it; he becomes one of them and thus is drawn into the scene.

- The purpose of placing human figures in an architectural drawing is to indicate scale.

- The placement of human figures can indicate spatial depth and levels.

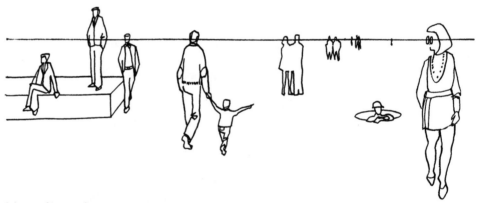

- The number, disposition, and dress of human figures can indicate usage of a space.

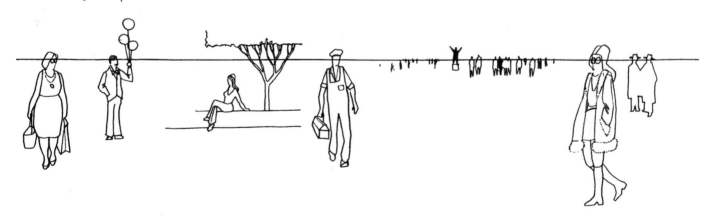

The important features of human figures, aside from their disposition, are:

- proportion;
- size; and
- attitude.

The human figure can be broken down into seven equal parts; the head is one-seventh of the total body weight.

It is generally easiest to start human figures with the head at eye level. In orthographic and paraline drawings the 5' – 6' height can be scaled. In perspectives the horizon line is at the viewer's eye level, so we can start at the horizon line. Figures above or below the level of the viewer can first be sized as if on the same level and then shifted up or down as required.

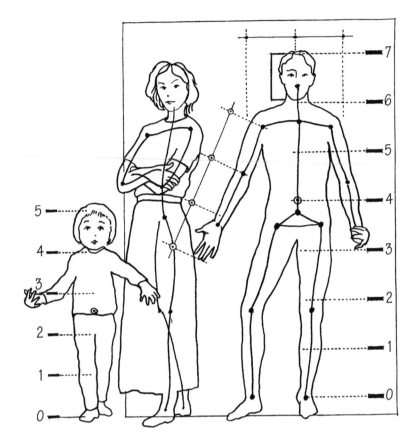

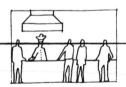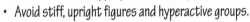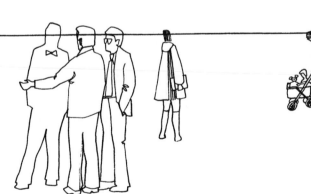

- Indicate activity appropriate to the space.
- Avoid stiff, upright figures and hyperactive groups.
- In composition, utilize both groups and solitary figures that are consistent with the usage of the space.

Figures can be abstractly outlined for use in a pure-line drawing
with shades of gray so as not to detract from the focus on the
architecture, or they can be given some detail that is consistent
with the scale, composition, and style of the drawing.

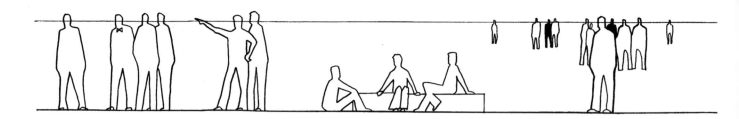

It is a good practice to collect and compile a file of magazine and
newspaper photographs of people and their activities to provide
tracers for various situations.

Be consistent: Each one of us inevitably develops his or her own
style of drawing.

Drawing furniture in conjunction with people helps to keep them in scale.

Keep furniture simple in plan.

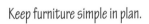

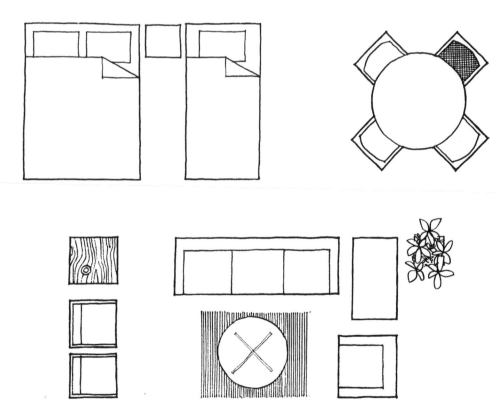

Be realistic with the placement — to indicate roadways and parking areas and the scale
— drawing cars in conjunction with people helps to keep them in scale.

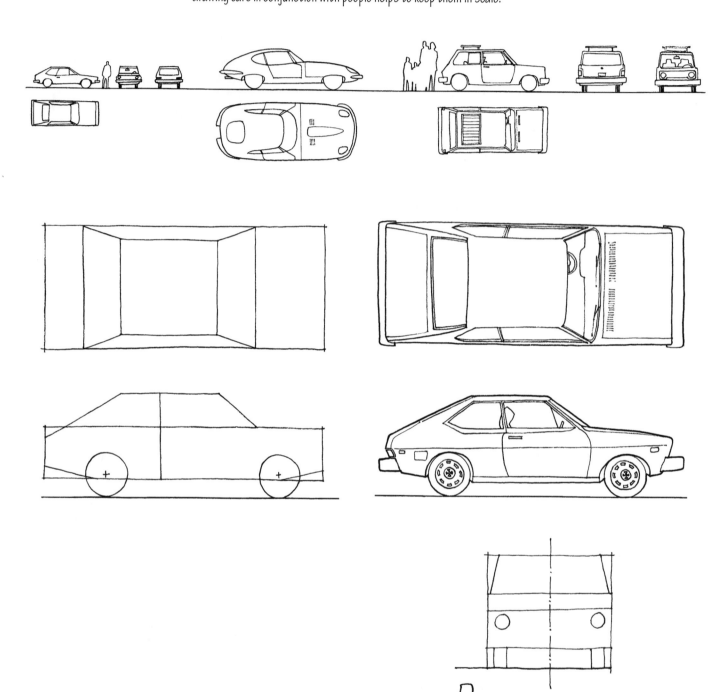

In addition to indicating *scale*, trees, landscaping, and ground patterns portray the *character* of a site, whether hilly or flat, wooded or barren, urban or rural, and are important means of providing *value contrast* in a drawing.

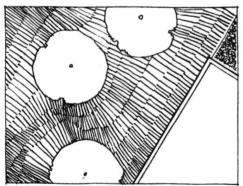
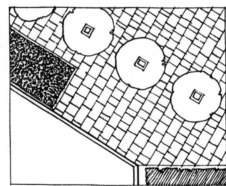

Entourage should never compete with but rather act as a foil for the architecture that is being illustrated.

Be economical. The style of an architectural drawing should be consistent throughout: Freehand entourage in a freehand drawing; hard-line entourage (abstracted as required) in a hard-line drawing. The amount of detail rendered should be consistent with the scale of the drawing.

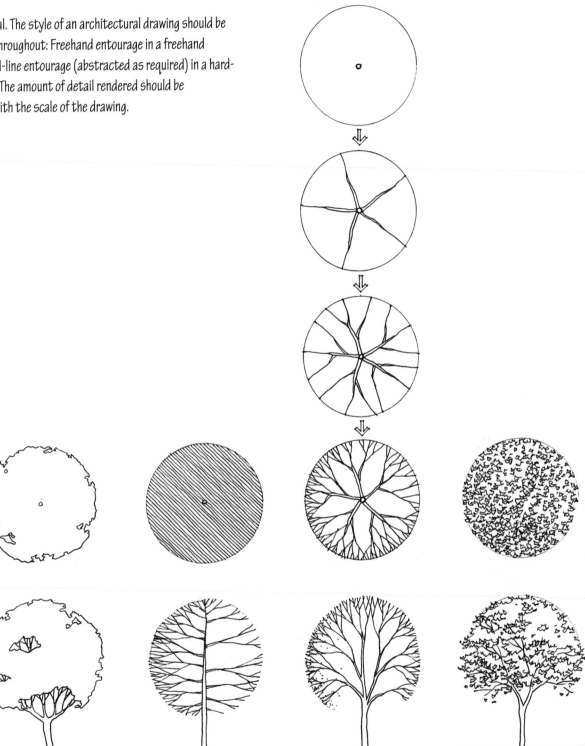

The type of foliage used in an architectural drawing should be appropriate to
the geographical location of the architecture.

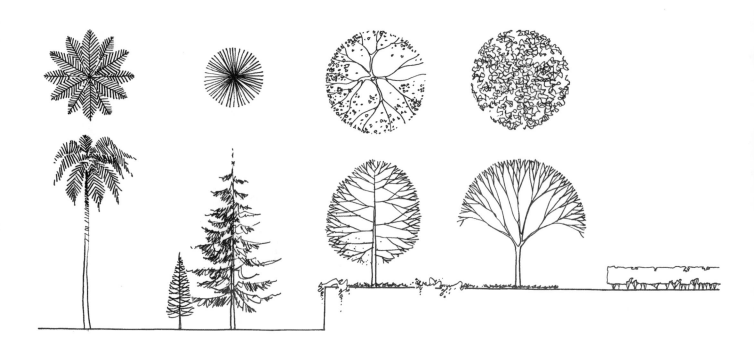

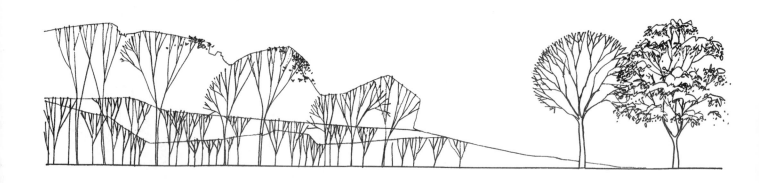

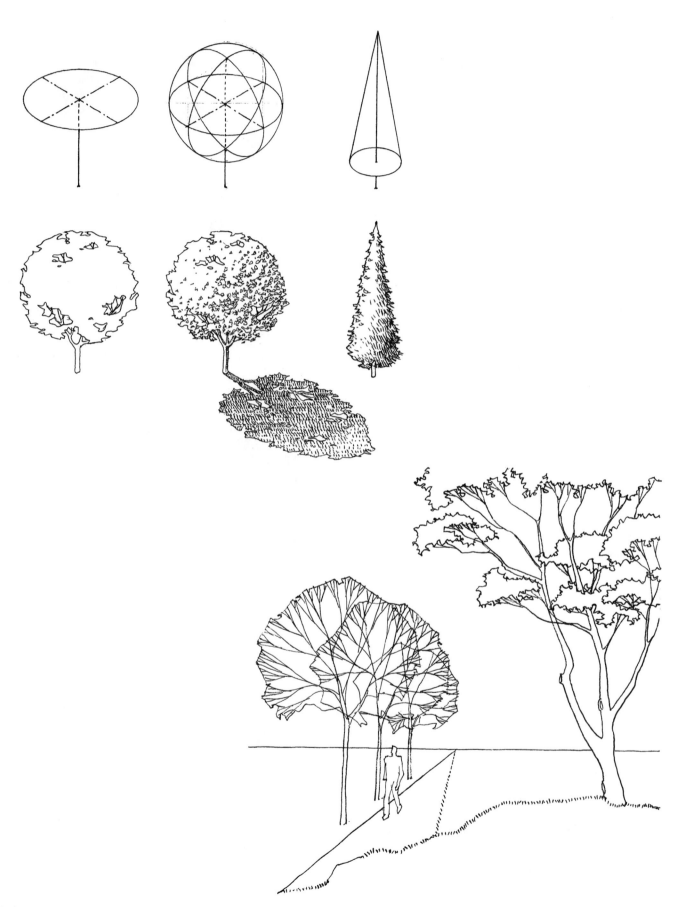

Entourage in foreground requires more detail but should not distract or draw attention away from the proper focus of an architectural drawing.

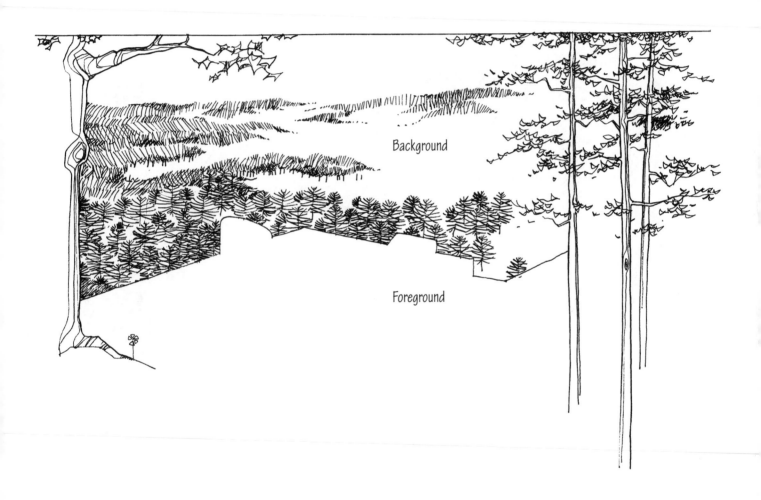

Background

Foreground

The tonal value (grayness) of a ground-plane texture should provide
the degree of contrast required to define the appropriate relationship
between adjacent forms.

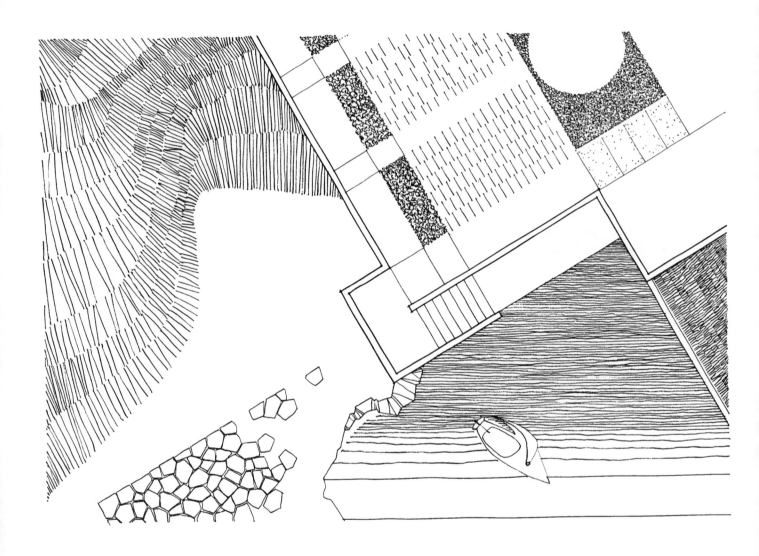

Everything that appears in front of or above a reflecting surface (glass, water, plastic, etc.) appears in back of or below the reflecting surface in a direction perpendicular to the surface (vertically or toward a vanishing point). Objects appear at the same distance in back of or below the reflecting surface as they do in front of or above that surface (see page 85).

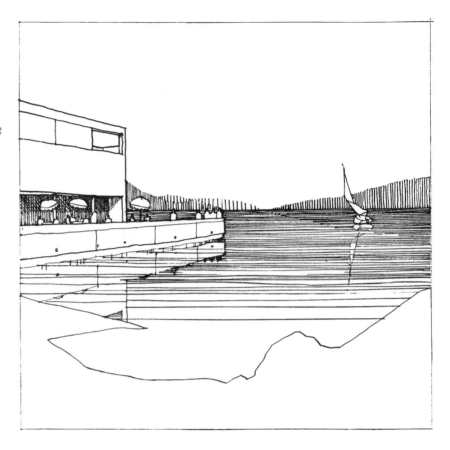

Water should be rendered as a *horizontal* planar surface. Use essentially *horizontal* lines—drafted for still water; freehand, wavy lines for ripply water.

Surfaces that are light in value appear lighter than the value of the water. Likewise, darker surfaces appear darker in reflection than the value of the water's surface.

The actual values you use for the reflecting surface, as well as the reflections within the surface area, should be determined relative to the range of values for the rest of the drawing.

Line drawing, no tones

Dark, still surface

Medium value, rippled surface

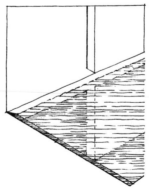

Light surface, receiving light

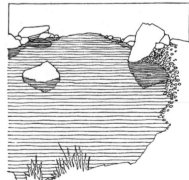

Light value, still water

5
Graphic Symbols
& Lettering

This chapter discusses graphic symbols and lettering, which help the viewer to identify and orient himself to the various architectural drawing elements that comprise a presentation. In enhancing the clarity and readability of architectural drawings, these devices become important elements in the overall composition of a presentation.

Graphic presentation symbols are conventions that rely on their graphic images to convey information. To be easily recognizable and readable, these images should be kept simple and clean (i.e., free of extraneous stylization).

north arrows

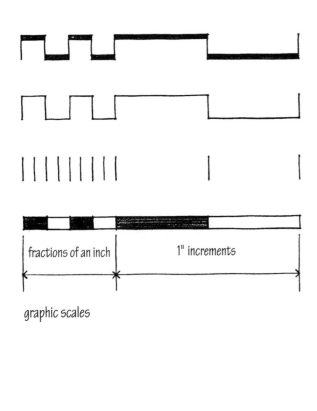

fractions of an inch | 1" increments

graphic scales

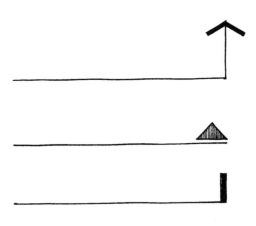

section arrows

elevation mark

boundary lines/
lines of emphasis

All graphic presentation symbols and lettering must be considered elements in the composition of a presentation. Their impact on the composition is dependent on their size, weight, and placement.

Size   should be determined on the basis of:

1. readability from the observer's point of view; and

2. the proportional relationship of the graphic symbols or lettering to the overall size and scale of the drawing.

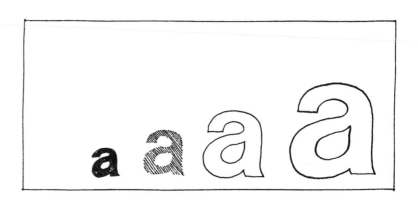

Weight   is determined by the size and value (ranging from white through a series of grays to black) of the graphic symbols or letters; i.e., if a large-sized typeface is required for readability from a certain distance, but a low value is mandatory for a balanced composition, then an outline letter should be used.

Placement   of titles and graphic symbols should be determined on the basis of their overall weight or tonal value and their role in the organization of the presentation.

The use of guidelines is mandatory for letters to be consistent in height.

ABCDEFGHIJKLMNOPQRRSTUVWXYZ   1234567890
ABCDEFGHIJKLMNOPQRRSTUVWXYZ   1234567890

For letters to communicate and not to distract or detract from the drawing itself:

1. Keep lettering vertical; a small triangle is a quick and efficient way to keep vertical lettering strokes consistently vertical.

    Slanted lettering is directional; this movement is generally distracting in a rectilinear drawing scheme.

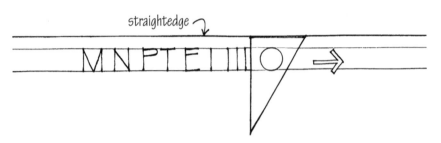

2. Maintain oblong proportions for the most stable lettering.

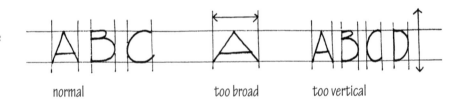

normal   too broad   too vertical

Everyone inevitably develops an individual style of lettering. The most important characteristics of a lettering style are readability and consistency, in both style and spacing.

Letter spacing is not based on equal spacing between the extremities of the letters but on equal areas.

equal areas correct   equal spacing incorrect

lowercase lettering can be appropriate if it is sympathetic to the drawing style and if it is executed consistently throughout the presentation. It is generally easy to read, because we recognize the distinctive differences among the characters from its widespread use in the printing industry.

abcdefgghijklmnopqrstuvwxyz

SERIFS enhance the recognition and readability of an alphabet. They too should be used consistently. Perhaps the best example of the use of serifs is the classic roman alphabet, which is the model for the single-stroke alphabet below:

serifs

ABCDEFGHIJKLMNOPQRSTUVWXYZ · 1234567890

The maximum-sized single-stroke letter or numeral that should be used is 3/16". Beyond this size a letter or numeral should have width and substance to its strokes so it doesn't appear too weak.

With the wealth of well-designed alphabets and typefaces available, you should not spend time designing new ones but rather learn when and where to utilize the existing ones. For this purpose, a press-on lettering catalog is excellent source material.

The character of the typeface used in the verbal supplement to the graphic presentation should be appropriate to the architecture being presented. The typeface can be consistent with the architectural style, or it can act as a foil or counterpoint to the subject matter.

The following page shows some representative typefaces.

HELVETICA MEDIUM · ABC · abc 123

Helvetica medium is a relatively neutral, well-proportioned alphabet; other sans serif (without serifs) alphabets are:

- folio medium
- standard medium
- univers 53
- venus medium

Lighter in weight and more elegant in character are:

- folio light
- helvetica light
- microgramma medium extended
- copperplate gothic
- optima stemple

A few sans serif alphabets with relatively heavy weight are:

- folio bold
- helvetica bold
- microgramma bold extended
- univers 75

Similar in weight but with serifs are:

- clarendon bold
- fortune bold (and extra bold)
- windsor bold

ABCDEFGHIJKLMNOPQRST
UVWXYZ & 1234567890

6
Freehand Drawing

This chapter first discusses the technique of sketching from real life, an invaluable exercise that enables you to develop the skill to portray graphically a condition or idea quickly and accurately and at the same time forces you to observe and analyze your environment. The second part discusses the use of graphic diagraming in the design process as an important communication device for the designer.

As a beginning student, you should whenever possible take the opportunity to sketch from real life to develop your drawing skills and sharpen your awareness of the existing environment. While sketching, you should not concentrate merely on drawing technique, or you will lose sight of what you see. Sketching from life trains you to observe, analyze, and evaluate while recording your environment.

The subject matter that you record should range in scale from the general to the specific. You should look at how pieces of the environment fit together; how the built environment relates to the natural; how elements of the environment juxtapose themselves; how buildings define exterior space, frame vistas, form walls or horizontal planes; how some buildings are in fact objects in space, while others form backgrounds for various elements. Of course, you are always concerned with form, light, texture, and space.

Look at individual buildings. Why do some have character and others do not? Investigate the physical elements that make up buildings. Look at details: how doors and windows are constructed, how brick walls turn corners, how various materials meet.

Observation and investigation, properly evaluated, help to build up your vocabulary of the environment, which will serve as a basis for much of what you do in the design studio.

The finished sketch should communicate your observations and your point of view. Just as your hand should be able to record graphically your observations quickly and accurately, your eye should be able to grasp quickly and accurately the nature of those observations. Beginning students often have difficulty in sketching accurately, since they believe they can comprehend without careful observation, confusing psychological impressions in the mind with what they really see. Although the merits of impressionistic sketches are arguable, when the accuracy of a sketch deteriorates to the point of being incomprehensible to the viewer, the communicative power of the graphics is lost.

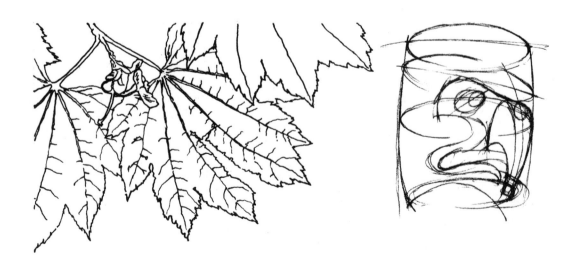

A variety of drawing instruments is available to the sketcher. At the start, you are encouraged to try all of the following: a soft pencil, HB or softer; a fountain pen with black ink; a black fiber-tip pen; a charcoal pencil; black and gray markers.

Experiment with the feel of each of these on various types of paper. Try to determine the limits of expression each is capable of and how its characteristics affect the nature of a sketch. For example, you should find that with a fine point you are capable of executing a variety of line types and further, that a pen-and-ink drawing consists mainly of lines. On the other hand, with a soft pencil or charcoal, you should be able to execute softer, more subtle lines and tones.

It should be noted that the width of a line (as determined by the drawing instrument you are using) determines how abstract or detailed a sketch can be. Drawing with a fine-point fountain pen encourage you to sketch in minute details. Since it takes innumerable fine ink lines to cover a given area, many fine ink-line drawings end up smaller than intended or, if large in size, weak in intensity. On the other hand, sketching with a marker forces you to look at and record broader lines and to eliminate details.

Sketches can consist purely of lines, or they can be combinations of line and tone, but the line remains the single most essential drawing element, since it is capable of such a wide range of expression. It can define shape and form and even imply a sense of depth and space. A line can portray hard as well as soft materials; it can be light or heavy, limp or taut, bold or tentative.

The following (through page 157) are examples of sketches, ranging in scale, subject matter, and technique.

A knowledge of the principles of perspective is indispensable for the sketching of architectural forms.

Although a line drawing can be informative, a sketch can also have tonal and textural interest.

Graphic diagrams, because of the visual thinking they stimulate, are an important tool of the designer. Graphic diagrams are visual abstractions that depict the essence of:

1. concepts (ideas, processes, events); and

2. objects (physical elements varying in scale).

The act of diagraming various aspects of an architectural idea enables a designer to investigate and communicate at a very general level the overall organization of a scheme, both two-dimensionally and three-dimensionally. A graphic portrayal of a building's organization through diagrams can be helpful not only in enhancing and keying the viewer's understanding of the normal architectural presentation drawings but also in enabling the designer to keep sight of his original intent during the design process. An excellent and clear concept is often obscured if not destroyed in the process of a design proposal's refinement and resolution in detail.

Some of the aspects of a building that can be effectively diagramed are:

1. functional zoning (horizontal and vertical);

2. zoning of degrees of privacy;

3. circulation (horizontal and vertical);

4. site conditions and context;

5. spatial hierarchy and relationships;

6. geometric properties;

7. lighting conditions (natural and artificial); and

8. structure and enclosure.

There are others, of course. It should be remembered that two-dimensional diagrams can communicate not only organizational ideas but also the implications of form.

Technique and media can vary from very loose, amorphous, freehand sketches (doodles) to precise, hard-line images.

Your choice of drawing equipment depends on the scale, the degree of abstraction, and the amount of detail.

In working from the general to the particular, from broad, overriding issues to a problem's resolution in detail, you are involved in abstraction, in separating the essential matter from more superficial concerns. Paralleling the gradual formulation, refinement, and crystallization of a problem (and the corresponding synthesis of given information and feedback), graphic technique progresses from generalized sketches, executed in broad strokes, to more definitive symbols of concrete ideas and solutions, executed with more precise instruments.

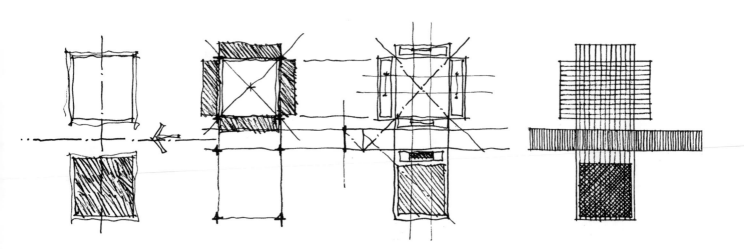

Zoning

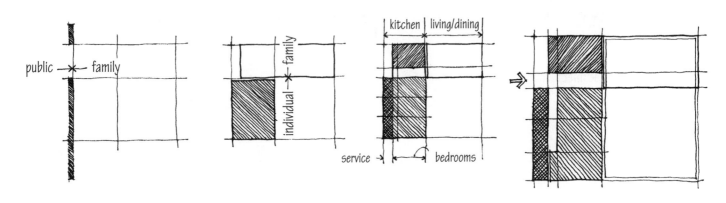

public → ✕ ← family

kitchen | living/dining

individual → ✕ ← family

service → | bedrooms

Circulation

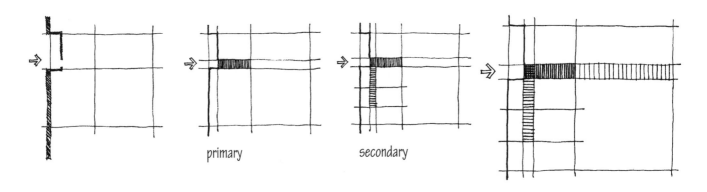

primary   secondary

Enclosure

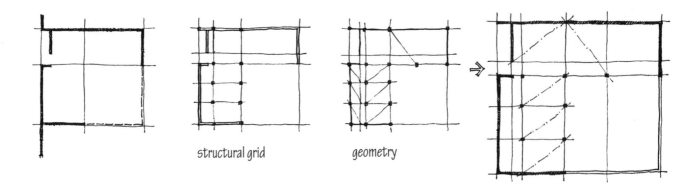

structural grid   geometry

Volumetric Study

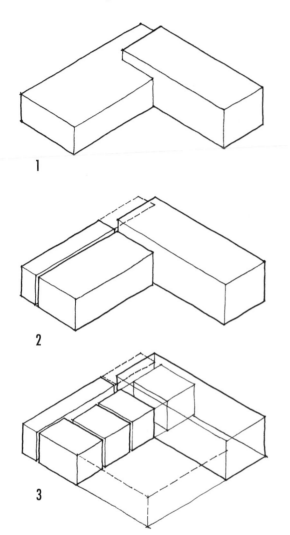

1

2

3

Section studies of bedroom wing

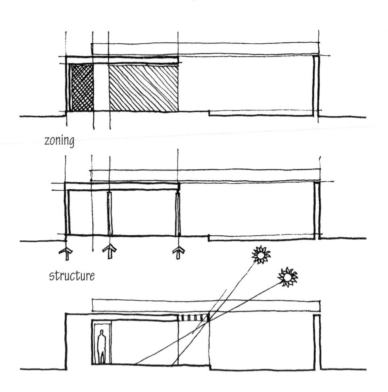

zoning

structure

Preliminary study of living-room space

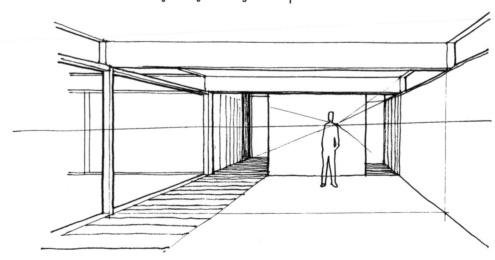

A well-developed ability to sketch enables a designer to investigate a number of alternatives quickly, accurately, and efficiently. With a roll of inexpensive yellow tracing paper and a soft pencil or marker, you should be able to start with a basic idea or scheme and, by a series of overlays and transformations, arrive at a number of reasonable alternatives. Every drawing or sketch along the way—whether the ideas it represents are accepted or rejected—helps you to gain further insight into the problem and often generates new ideas while enhancing the chances of cross-fertilization among any number of previous ideas.

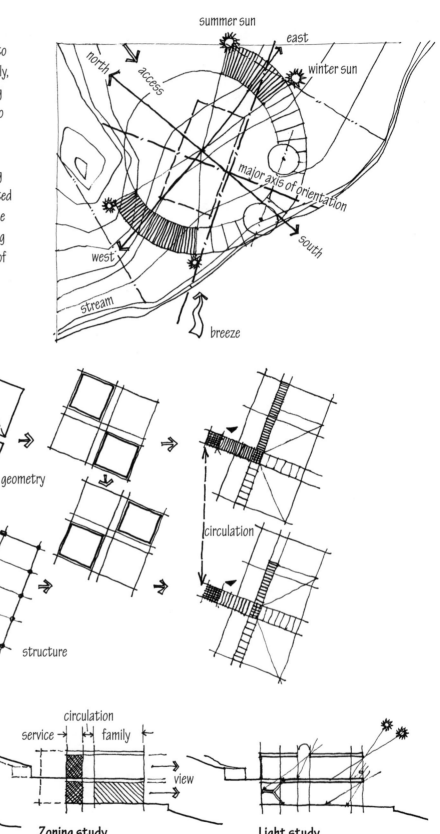

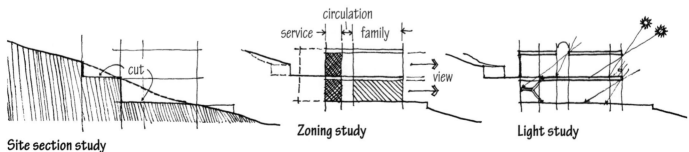

Site section study

Zoning study

Light study

Preliminary study for living-room space

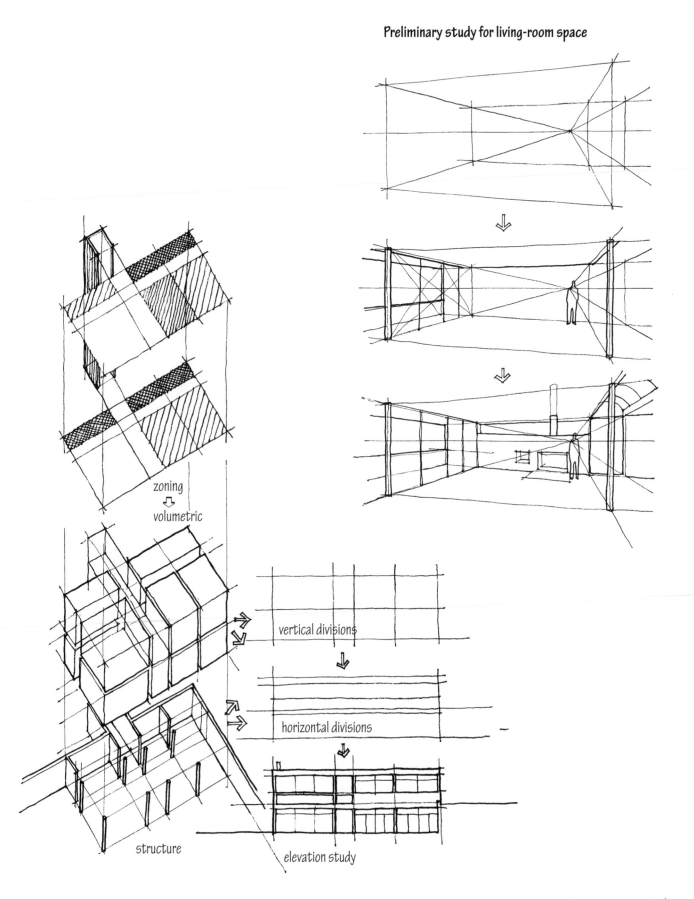

zoning
volumetric

vertical divisions

horizontal divisions

structure

elevation study

7
Architectural Presentations

The primary purpose of architectural graphics is communication. Although the drawings that comprise an architectural presentation may be excellent two-dimensional graphics worthy of an exhibition, they are merely communicative tools, never primary ends in themselves.

An architectural presentation's drawings are its primary meanings of communication. Unless the architectural drawings and graphics are comprehensible—their conventions understood and their substance meaningful—the presentation will be weak and ineffective. An effective presentation, however, also possesses collective characteristics, which can enhance the readability of the drawings themselves:

1. A point of view: A presentation should communicate the central idea of a design scheme—graphic diagrams/abstractions/overlays are effective means of articulating the various aspects of a design scheme, especially when they are visually related to the more common architectural drawings.

2. Unity: In an effective presentation no one segment is inconsistent with or detracts from the whole.

Unity (not to be confused with uniformity) depends on:
- a logical and comprehensible arrangement of integrated graphic and verbal information; and
- a consistent scale/format/medium/technique synthesis appropriate to the design as well as to the place and audience for which the presentation is intended.

3. Continuity: Each segment of a presentation should relate to what precedes and what follows it, reinforcing all the other segments of the presentation.

The principles of unity and continuity are mutually self-supporting; one cannot be achieved without the other; the factors that produce one invariably reinforce the other. At the same time, however, emphasis on your central idea can be brought into focus through the placement and pacing of the major and supporting graphic and verbal elements that comprise the presentation.

4. Efficiency: An effective presentation employs economy of means, utilizing only what is necessary to communicate an idea; if the graphic elements of a presentation become overly demonstrative and ends in themselves, the intent and purpose of the presentation are obscured.

The composition and arrangement of the following elements must be considered in any architectural presentation:

- Graphic images: architectural drawings
  graphic diagrams
- Graphic/verbal information: north arrows, graphic scales, etc.
  titles, legends, etc.
- Field/ground relationship: white/gray/colored residual spaces

All of these elements have the following properties, which must be considered in composing a visually balanced presentation:

- Shape
- Size ⎤
       ⎬ Weight
- Value ⎦
- Placement: direction / attitude / interval

Architectural presentations generally read from left to right and from top to bottom, except in the case of a slide presentation, which involves a sequence in time. The subject matter presented should progress from the general or contextual view to the specific, as illustrated on the following page.

Paraline and perspective drawings should relate as directly as possible to their contextual drawing.

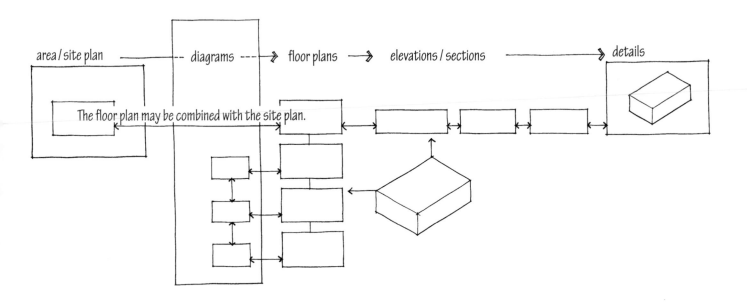

area / site plan ----- diagrams ---> floor plans ---> elevations / sections ------> details

The floor plan may be combined with the site plan.

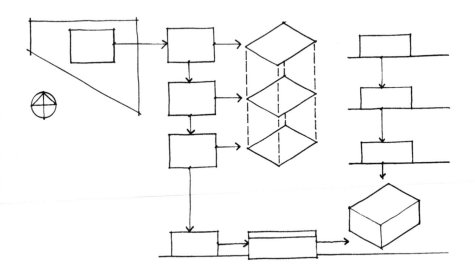

All plans (site/floor/diagrammatic) should be oriented in a similar manner.

Whenever possible, orient plans with north up or upward.

Floor plans of multistory buildings should relate vertically or horizontally, preferably along their long sides.

Building elevations should proceed vertically or horizontally from the floor plans.

Likewise, building sections should relate either vertically or horizontally to the floor plans or the building elevations.

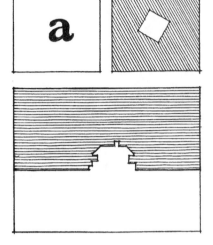 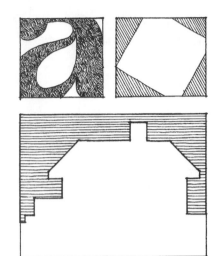

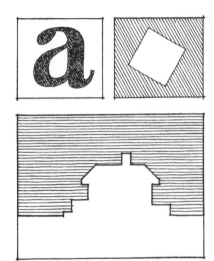

The size of a graphic image relative to the size of its field determines how the figure is read. When situated in a large field, its individuality is enhanced.

If the figure is enlarged relative to its field, it begins to interact visually with it. The field begins to have a recognizable shape or figural quality of its own.

If the figure is enlarged still further, an ambiguous figure-ground relationship is established in which the field elements can also be seen as figures.

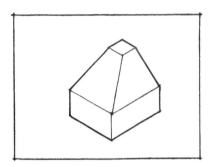 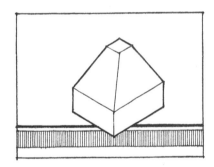 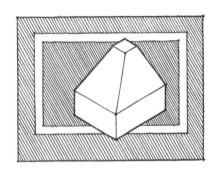

When a paraline or perspective drawing without a rectilinear shape floats in a field for emphasis,

it can be stabilized visually with either a title block or horizontal band.

When framing or matting a drawing, avoid using a double or triple mat. Doing so can create the impression of a figure on a background that itself has a background. Attention, therefore, would be diverted from the figure, where it belongs, to the frame around it.

Architectural drawings are often presented as groups of figures. A series of plans for a multistory building or a set of elevations are the most typical examples. The spacing and alignment of these individual drawings, as well as similarity of shape and treatment, are the key factors in determining whether these drawings are to be read as a set or as individual figures.

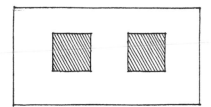 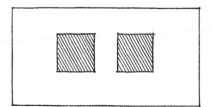 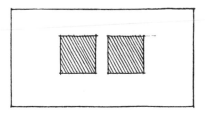

If two drawings are to be read as individual figures, the space between them should be equal to the space between each drawing and the edge of the field.

If moved closer together, the drawings begin to be read more as a related group.

If moved closer still, the drawings read more as a single view rather than as two individual views.

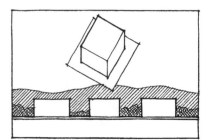 

Properly related drawings that form a set can themselves define an edge of a field for another drawing or set of figures.

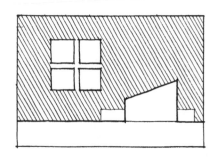 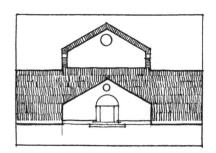 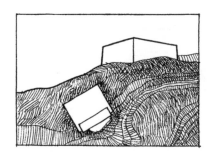

Introducing a tonal value to a drawing field can aid in defining a field within a larger field. A darker background for an elevation drawing can merge with a section drawing. The foreground for a perspective can become the field for a plan view of the building.

Lettering in an architectural presentation should be carefully integrated into the composition of drawings on each board or panel. Clarity is the goal. Use the simplest, most efficient letterform possible.

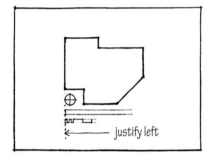

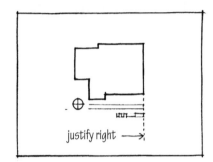

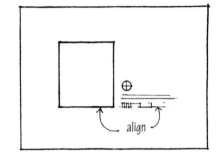

Titles for drawings and graphic symbols that identify and explain the contents of a specific drawing should be related directly to that drawing and be clearly a part of the drawn zone.

Lettering should be organized into sets of information. Relate these sets directly to the portion of the drawing to which they refer.

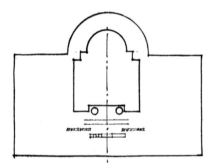

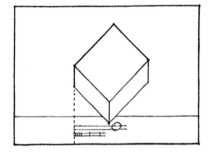

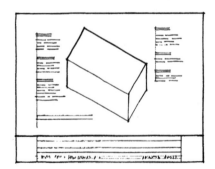

A symmetrical layout is best used with symmetrical drawings.

Titles for drawings can help stabilize odd-shaped drawings.

The project title and associated information should not relate to any single drawing but to the overall board or panel.

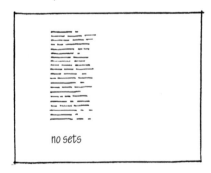

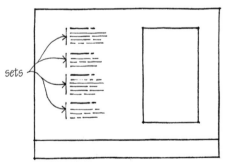

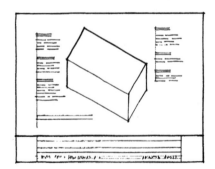

Text should be organized into visual sets of information. The space between lines of text should be at least one-half of the letter height used. The space between sets of information should be at least equal to the height of two lines of text.

The range of letter sizes used should be determined by the distance from which the audience will view the presentation. Different portions of a presentation—overviews, diagrams, details, text, etc.—may be read at different distances.

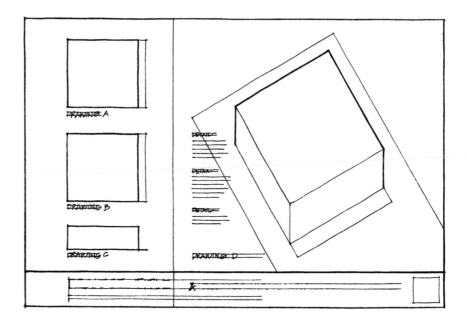

If you wish the panels to be displayed in a specific manner, you may use a more graphic means to identify the relative position of each panel in the display.

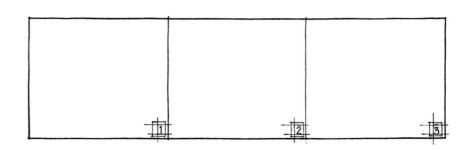

When a presentation consists of more than one panel or board, each panel or board may be identified by a number. This information should be in the same relative position on each board.

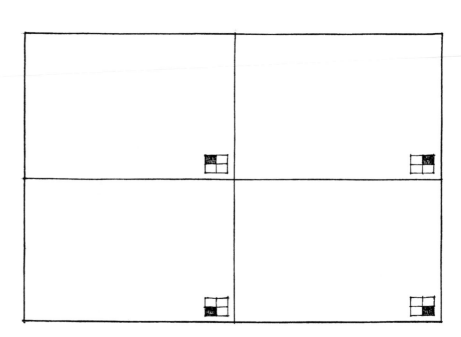

A set of related drawings may be laid out in a vertical, horizontal, or grid format.

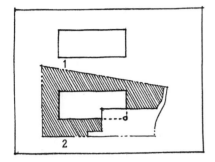

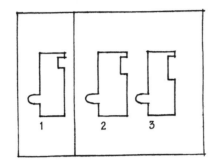

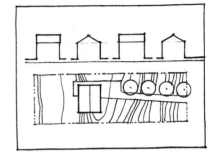

Plan drawings may be related vertically or horizontally, preferably along their long dimension.

Elevation and section drawings also may be related vertically, although they more often are displayed horizontally.

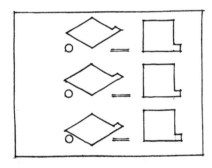

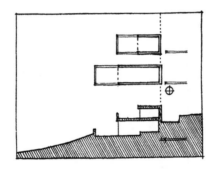

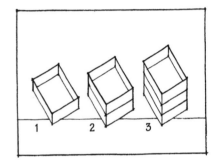

Plan drawings can be related to paraline views horizontally,

or to section and elevation views vertically.

A series of paraline drawings may be laid out vertically, or horizontally where each drawing successively builds on the preceding one.

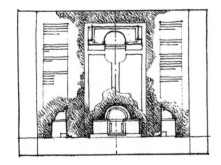

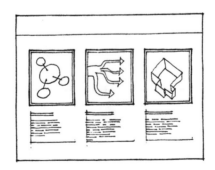

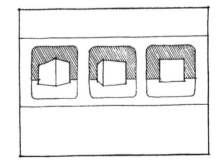

A symmetrical layout works best in presenting a symmetrical building design.

If a series of related drawings are of different types and/or treated in different ways, they may be unified by framing or boxing them in a uniform manner.

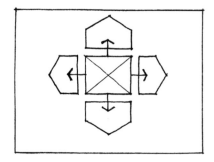
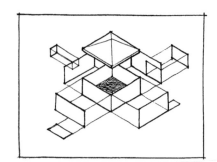
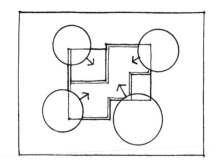

Centralized formats include a plan surrounded by elevation views, an expanded paraline drawing, and a key drawing surrounded by detailed portions drawn at a larger scale.

A grid provides the most flexibility for laying out a series of drawings and informational text on a panel or series of boards. The underlying sense of order created by the grid allows a great variety of information to be presented in a uniform manner.

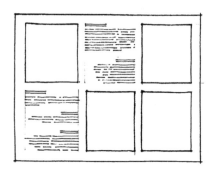
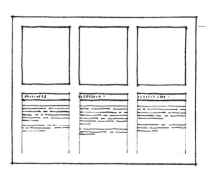

The grid may be square or rectangular.

Drawings, diagrams, and text may be displayed in individual boxes or frames.

Drawings may be displayed horizontally with text below to form columns.

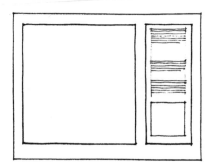
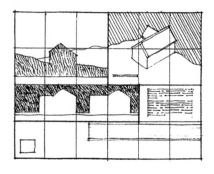
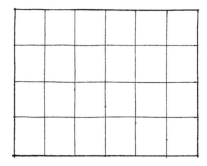

An important drawing may take up more than one box or frame.

Graphics and text may be integrated in an organic manner.

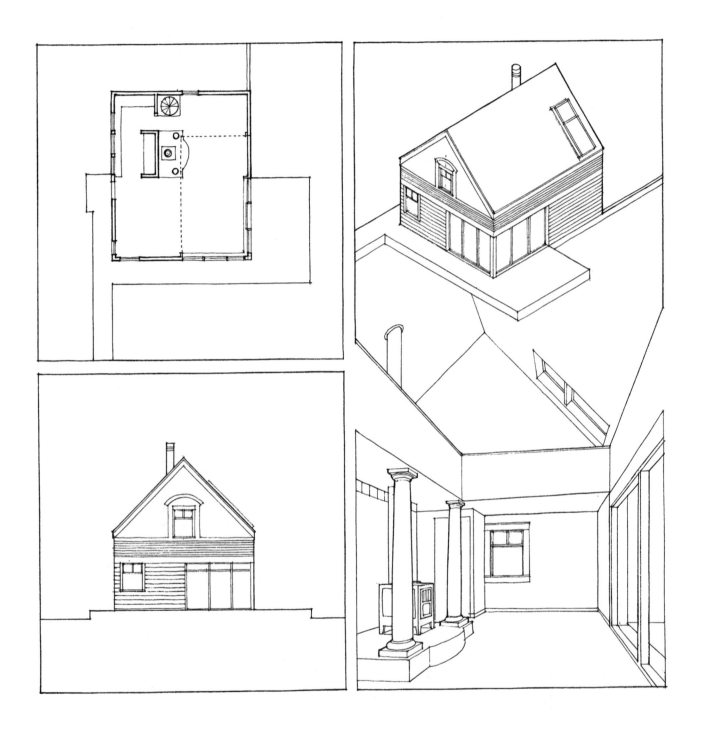

In conclusion, remember that drawing skills allow you to be eloquent, but you must first master the fundamentals. It takes discipline to draw a line, construct a perspective, or cast a shadow. It is hoped that this introduction to the basic elements of architectural graphics will provide you with a foundation upon which to build and develop the necessary physical and mental skills to communicate graphically with clarity and honesty.

"Art does not reproduce the visible; it renders visible." *Paul Klee*

INDEX

adjustable triangle 6

aerial views 78

architectural presentations 165–174

architect's scale 9

area plan 167

assumed north 30, 40

axonometric lines 48

bifold door 26

boundary lines 30, 146

brick 109

building elevations 40, 42, 101, 167

building cutaway 50

building details 24, 4150

building form 42, 49

building sections 19, 34–37, 100, 119, 167

cars 132–133

ceiling plans 29

centerlines 12

center of view 57

circles 15

    in paraline views 47, 50

    in perspective 84

circle template 7

circulation 160

compass 7

concept 158

concrete 108

concrete block 109

cone of vision 57

construction drawing 34, 39

context 127

continuity 165

contour drawings 90

contour interval 31

contour lines 31, 111

contrast 23, 28, 32–33, 37, 44, 91, 96, 98–107

convergence 55, 59

cutaway views 50, 52, 102

cut lines 22, 28, 35, 92

dash lines 12, 27

depth cues 42–43

design section 34, 39

diagonal point 67

diagonals in perspective 83

diagraming 158–163

diagrams 167

diminution of size 55

doors 26, 41, 108

dot pattern 97, 111

drafting brush 8

drafting technique 14

drawing board cover 10

drawing circles 15, 47, 50

drawing details 24–25

drawing ink 4

drawing layout 15, 20

drawing lead 3

drawing media 95

drawing pencil 2

drawing relationships 167, 172–173

drawing scale 9, 24–25, 35, 41

drawing surface 3

drawing techniques 92, 95, 159

drawing titles 170

dry transfer tints 95, 97

efficiency 166

electric eraser 8

elevation obliques 45, 46

elevations 17, 18, 40–44, 45, 101, 113, 115, 119, 167

ellipses 47

eraser 8

enclosure 160

engineer's scale 9

erasing shield 8

expanded views 51, 52–53, 102

exterior perspectives 78, 105

eye-level views 78

figure-ground relationships 168–169

floor plans 17, 19, 20–23, 29, 33, 99, 118, 167

focus 106–107, 139

foreshortening 55

fractional distance point 69

fractional measuring point 75

freeform curves 47

freehand drawing 152–157

French curve 7

furniture 131

glass 108, 142

graphic diagraming 158–163

graphic scales 146

graphic symbols 146–147

gray scale 97

grid layouts 173

grid lines 12, 28, 47

ground line 56, 58

ground plane 58, 140

handlettering 148–149

hidden lines 27

horizon line 56, 58, 70, 78

human figures 128–130

illustration board 10

interior perspectives 71, 79, 104, 107

interior plants 141

isometric drawings 45, 46

landscape 134

leadholder 2

lead weight 3

lettering 148–150

light 90, 104, 162

light rays 112

line and tone 92, 93, 95

line drawing 92, 93, 95

line of sight 56

line quality 13

line types 12
line weights 12, 22, 35, 36, 42, 51, 90–91

masonry 109
material patterns 99, 101, 108–111, 116
measuring points 73
mechanical pencil 2
metal roofing 111
multiview drawings 45

nonaxonometric lines 48
north arrows 30, 146

oblique drawings 45
one-point perspective 64, 65–71
optical illusion 48
orthographic projection 17, 18
orthographic drawings 45
overlapping 55

paneling 110
paraline drawings 45, 46–53, 102, 114, 161, 163
    shade and shadows 120
parallel rule 5
parallel stairs 27
pencil point 14
pencils 2
people 35, 128–130
perspective characteristics 54

perspective drawings 45, 54–64, 161, 163
perspective grid 69, 76–77
perspective sections 88, 103
perspective setup 57, 65, 72
perspective types 64
perspective variables 60–63, 68, 70, 78
pictorial views 45, 49
picture plane 56, 58
planar corners 93–94
plan obliques 45, 46
plan perspective 70
plans 17, 18, 29, 45, 46, 113, 115, 160, 162
    shade and shadows 119
pocket door 26
point of view 60–63, 165
presentation drawings 167
profile lines 35, 42, 51, 92, 100
property lines 12, 30, 146
pure-line drawing 92, 93, 95
pure tone 92, 94

reflected ceiling plans 29
reflected light 117
reflections 142–144
    in perspective 85–87
rendering 117
return stairs 27
revolving door 26
roofing 111
roof plans 17, 29, 32

scale 9, 24–25, 128, 134, 146

scribble technique 97, 111

section arrows 34–35, 146

section perspectives 88, 103

sections 17, 18, 34, 44, 45, 100, 161, 162

shade 93–94, 112

shade and shadows 112–117

    in plans and sections 118–119

    in paraline drawings 120–121

    in perspective 122–126

shade line 112

shadows 93–94, 112

shingles 111

single-view drawings 45

site analysis 162

site boundaries 30

site sections 38, 162

site orientation 30

site plans 30, 32–33, 98, 116, 167

site topography 31

sketching 152–157

sliding door 26

sloping lines in perspective 80–81

spatial edges 93–94

spiral stairs 27

stairs 27

stairs in perspective 82

station point 56, 57

stippling 97, 111

stone 109

straight-run stairs 27

structure 162, 163

subdivision in perspective 83

technical pen 4

texture 96, 101

three-point perspective 64

titling drawings 170

tonal values 23, 32, 37, 43–44, 90–91, 96, 98–107

tone of lines 92, 94, 95, 97

topography 31, 134

tracing paper 10

trees 134–139

triangles 6

true north 40

t-square 5

two point perspective 64, 72–79

typefaces 150

unity 165

vanishing points 56, 59, 73

views 103, 106–107

visual sets 169–170

volumetric study 161, 163

walls 28

water 85, 142–143

windows 26, 41, 108

wood siding 110

zoning 160, 162–163

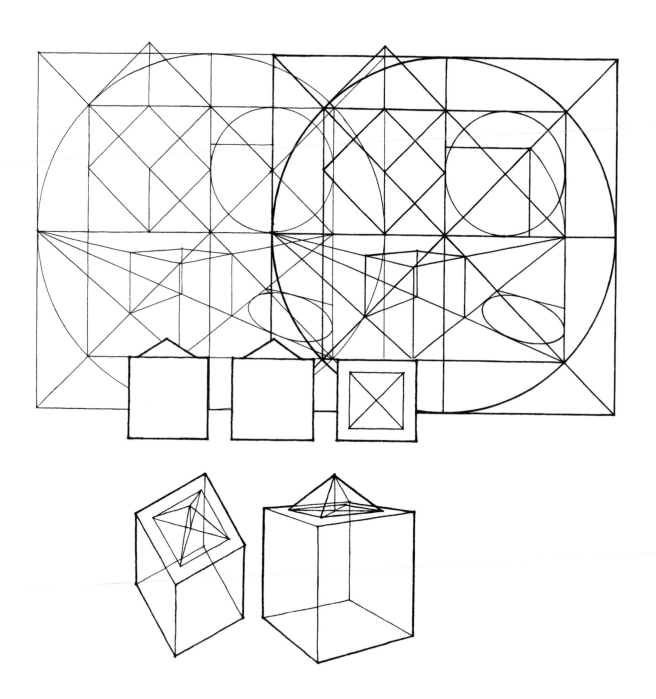